SECRETS
OF BEING A
HAPPY
CHURCH MEMBER

SECRETS
OF BEING A
HAPPY
CHURCH MEMBER

DR. TERRY CUTRER

WESTBOW
PRESS®
A DIVISION OF THOMAS NELSON
& ZONDERVAN

WestBow Press books may be ordered through booksellers or by contacting:

WestBow Press
A Division of Thomas Nelson & Zondervan
1663 Liberty Drive
Bloomington, IN 47403
www.westbowpress.com
844-714-3454

Scripture taken from the King James Version of the Bible.

ISBN: 978-1-6642-7069-5 (sc)
ISBN: 978-1-6642-7070-1 (hc)
ISBN: 978-1-6642-7068-8 (e)

Library of Congress Control Number: 2022912112

Print information available on the last page.

WestBow Press rev. date: 7/5/2022

CONTENTS

Through the years, one of the biggest sources of inspiration has been my three daughters: Carrie, Cassie, and Corrie. They have all three internalized their faith in Jesus and been productive, happy church members themselves. May they continue the quest and pass the torch to their children.

FOREWORD

I've known Terry Cutrer since we were in elementary school together. Through the years, I've found him to be one of the most thoughtful, gracious believers I've ever known. It was no surprise to those of us who knew Terry that God would call him into ministry. He has been a faithful servant of Christ for decades. The wisdom he brings in this book is the result of years of ministry.

If you've been around the church long, you know there are all kinds of people sitting in the pews. Some serve with joy. The folks who partner with their pastor in ministry, who have a heart for the lost in their community, and who model Christlike joy energize the church and the pastor. They find the journey through life to be filled with joy. Whether it's in their work, their church service, their family, or their daily disciplines, the fragrance of Christ is on their lives. They are the ones you want at the front door, greeting the visitors. They are the ones who give in every way they can to the vision. As I look over my ministry, God has always graced me with men and women who "got it" and partnered to give the church a witness in the community.

Then there are the others. They seem to sit, soak, and sour. They can find something wrong with everything. They don't enjoy the journey and really don't want anyone else to enjoy it. For some reason, they seem to have gotten saved, but gotten over it. They are in a rut, backslidden, or just stuck in wanting it to be their way. Often their mindset is "This is *my* church," and they are immediately skeptical of any new pastor, vision, or mission. As Warren Wiersbe said, there are those who think, *As long as I'm in this church, there will be no unanimous vote.*

Life is too short to not enjoy the journey. You may have picked this book up or had it given to you by a fellow believer. As you read it, it's imperative to take an honest look in the mirror. Does this book describe me? Have I lost my joy? Am I happy with where I am spiritually? Is there something that needs to change in my habits, attitudes, relationships? Maybe we need to get over ourselves. We must remember it's not our church; it's *His* church. He wants His body, His bride, to advance the kingdom.

How will we be remembered? Will they honor us when we pass from death to life as faithful servants? Or will we be remembered in a negative light? We get to choose. We can change. This is not rocket science. Pastor Terry Cutrer has written a book to help each of us be happy, joyful church members. Take time to read each chapter. Ask yourself, "Am I joyful? Am I one of those who finds joy in the journey?"

Don't be a church curmudgeon. Don't die a grouch. Don't waste your life. Be a blessing. Return to your first love. Remember the joy you felt when you were first saved, before you met too many sour Christians. Vance Havner said, "I like to meet a new believer before he runs into too many church members." Don't be that kind of church member. Be happy. Smile. Embrace all God has for you as a child of the King.

Michael Catt
Retired pastor, Sherwood Church
MichaelCatt.com
Executive producer, Sherwood Films
Founder ReFresh Conference

INTRODUCTION

Having pastored six churches with various backgrounds, economic levels, and locations, it has become obvious that in almost every church, there are those who get a charge out of their church life. Church is something that energizes these people. They are happier as a result of what they receive from the Lord through what He calls His body.

On the other hand, there are many church members who are flippant, unconcerned, or even antagonistic about their church life. *Happiness* and *joy* are not words they would associate with church. At one time, some of these may have known the exhilaration that can come from being a part of a church body, but that is no longer there. This person may be as involved as ever, or he may have dropped out of church completely. In either case, there is not happiness coming as a result of his relationship with his church. This book is addressed to those millions who want the joy of their church life, as well as their salvation, restored.

1

PARTICIPATION

For a member of the body to ensure happiness in the church, he or she needs to have some areas of participation. This could be teaching a weekly class, singing in a choir, telephoning the elderly, and participating in other activities that need to be done routinely to be effective. On the other hand, there need to be areas of spontaneous service. These are one-time events rather than weekly or monthly commitments, such as helping someone fix a flat tire on the side of the road, taking a meal to parents of a new baby, or helping someone who has fallen at the store.

There are some situations when both of these areas of service come together. This first hit me as a young pastor who was learning to prepare weekly sermons. Early in my ministry, it became apparent one of the best uses of my time was to adequately prepare each week to preach the Word of God. There was a time I honestly thought that with the Holy Spirit's leading, and with four years of college and three years of seminary, great sermons would just flow. This was not the case. In fact, it took me several hours to adequately prepare. Consistency was key to seeing a sermon come to fruition.

Then there were times when, even with proper preparation, I would enter the pulpit feeling dry. It was after one of those sermons that I recalled a comment by Dr. Robert Naylor, a former president of Southwestern Baptist Theological Seminary. He told of times as a pastor when his sermon for the coming Sunday was just dry, even after pouring over it. His remedy was to do something spontaneous for Jesus, like going to visit prospects on Saturday evening. It was after this contact with those who needed a walk with Jesus, and especially when they accepted the Lord, that he would again experience power in his preaching.

My situation was much the same. There were sermons that, even after good preparation, seemed stiff and lackluster. It was then that I purposely went out and sought to spontaneously do something for Jesus. Then the holy unction of the Spirit would often take place. Over the years, it has become obvious that good sermons typically take both consistent and spontaneous participation for them to be all they should be. The same is true in every Christian's life. Consistency and spontaneity are both important for happiness.

CONSISTENT PARTICIPATION: FILLING THE NECESSARY SLOTS

One of the biggest tasks churches face on an annual basis is that of filling all the positions that enable a church to function consistently. Sunday school teachers, ushers, choir leaders, committee or team members, security personnel, and more need to be selected so the work of the church can be continued. Filling these positions can often be a lengthy process, and many times is very arduous. Yet doing so is a God-given task that needs to be taken seriously. In 1 Corinthians 12:7, we find "the manifestation of the Spirit is given to every man to profit withal." More than just matching names with slots to be filled, those responsible for these selections need to remember that the productivity of the church as a whole, the ability of individual members to exercise their God-given gifts and abilities, and even the potential for members to know joy and happiness in their church membership is at stake. More along these lines will be discussed in the next chapter.

There is a story from a few years ago that explains the necessity of those selecting people for individual service positions being sensitive to the gifts of their fellow church members. A church was developing its broadcast capabilities to better reach potential viewers of the Sunday morning worship time. The volunteers serving in the broadcast booth had reached their limits as far as what they were able to do. They knew more equipment needed to be purchased, yet these volunteers were not sure what the best purchases would be. Further, they did not have the knowledge to operate anything beyond what they already had.

The pastor decided to go to a local television station and ask the manager if he knew of anyone who could help, even if it meant paying an expert for his time. The manager smiled a bit and then told the pastor that the best man in the city to do the job was a member in that very church. He was helping direct parking on Sunday mornings!

No one in the selection process, including the pastor, knew the capabilities of this man. When contacted, he was more than willing to help and add his expertise to rectify the situation in the broadcast booth. Such stories show how important it is that a selection committee do a thorough job of knowing the individuals in a church and connect them to areas where their gifts are best used. The result is a much happier church member and a more effective church.

We know from 1 Corinthians 12:11 and 18 that every believer has been endowed with at least one spiritual gift and that the Holy Spirit chooses who is to be endowed with what abilities. This means that every member has something to contribute to the uplifting of the body of Christ. Many have unique contributions to make. Yet because of the organizational structure of most churches, channels are not always available for these gifts to be used properly. Everyone is not equipped for the obvious tasks, such as teaching a class or working with youth. For organization's sake, people's abilities and gifts are often made to fit into a program instead of the programs being tailored to the abilities of a gifted individual member.

PROBLEMS IN CONSISTENT SERVICE

What can easily happen is that people who want to serve are funneled into the church's organizational structure. The church becomes guilty of simply keeping its organizations running smoothly instead of looking to see what gifts the Lord has given to the members and how best to use them. People will never feel the full satisfaction of knowing that they are in the center of God's will until they are using the God-given abilities at their disposal. It is up to churches to allow members the opportunity to use what they have. There is no need to make them miserable by forcing them into positions for which they are not well-suited or gifted.

At a former church, there was an older widow who visited and soon joined. Those who knew her age would call her elderly, but not those who knew her energy level. Her life had not been easy in any respect, having been a single parent for much of her life. Still, she had a strong faith in the Lord's willingness and ability to work in and through her. At the same time, she was open about her limitations; she had poor eyesight, she did not feel comfortable singing in public, and she could only occasionally help with the nursery. Finding a place of service for this pleasant and determined lady proved to be very difficult.

One day she came to me with an idea. She wanted to know if she could teach a Bible study class at an assisted living facility just a block from where she lived. This was surprising because she was older than half the residents. She was insistent though, so we went to the administration of the facility, and they were willing to give it a try. After visiting with some of the patients and drumming up some interest, we had the first meeting. Since she had never done this before, she asked me to teach the first lesson. After that, she ran me out and took over the program. Within a few weeks, she shared the gospel with those attending the Bible study and saw four people respond. She developed relationships and gave encouragement as few people could. It was one of those situations in which both the teacher and students were blessed.

Because of our church's structure, we almost missed an opportunity for helping our community, for blessing this lady with using what she had, and for encouraging a group of forgotten people who needed desperately to be remembered. We were able to find a place of service for someone even though it was not on the list of jobs. When church leaders look beyond organizational charts to the members themselves, more possibilities exist to help church members serve. This enables everyone to have greater happiness.

SPONTANEOUS PARTICIPATION

An interesting characteristic of those who have a high happiness level in their church life is that they often have times of spontaneity in their service. They have their loins girded so as to be ready soldiers whenever they may be called into action. There are instances of service in their lives that are not just regular, repeated, organized occurrences. Time is taken to help in ways and manners that are not totally planned and that are basically a one-shot happening. These church members are not so wrapped up in daily schedules that they cannot be open to something that is unplanned but still significant.

In the Old Testament, there are significant instances in which a person took time to help another on the spur of the moment. Perhaps the most notable and influential centers around the time Rebekah met Abraham's servant at the well. In Genesis 24:10, we are told this servant was traveling with ten camels as he searched for a wife for his master's son, Isaac. So he would know the right young lady to choose as Isaac's bride, this servant prayed for a rather unusual sign: the one he sought would offer water to him and to his ten thirsty camels as well. When Rebekah appeared on the scene, she did indeed offer to provide water for the traveling stranger as well as his camels.

This spontaneous act of generous kindness on Rebekah's part reveals her true character. The servant was not looking for just any sign from God; he was looking for something that would reveal a strong inner character.

Happy church members realize that the Lord has special areas of service awaiting those with open eyes as they go through their daily schedules. There will be unplanned and often unusual areas of service for those who are looking. Yet most church members miss out on the happiness that comes from spontaneous service.

PROBLEMS WITH SPONTANEOUS SERVICE

Problem 1: Fear

One big problem that occurs, especially in larger, urban areas, is the fear of being harmed because of helping others. There is indeed a certain risk when one attempts to help others, especially strangers. It is this vulnerability that scares off many from spontaneous service. Personal security is one of people's primary concerns, and often justly so. Some situations warrant extreme caution, but we all encounter viable situations for helping others every week.

What also needs to be remembered is a point from the parable of the Good Samaritan. The Samaritan took some *big* risks in helping the man on the side of the road. Who was to say that the thieves who had beaten this man were gone? Or if they had left, would they return to rob and beat the Samaritan? When the Samaritan arrived at the inn, he paid for the lodging of the beaten man and promised further payment if required. What if the inn keeper cheated him?

From all indications, the beaten man was Jewish and perhaps would show no appreciation because of the differences and rivalry between the two nationalities. With all the risks involved, the Samaritan still took time to give spontaneous service.

There are times when certain risks have to be waived in view of the needs of others. Can a Christian idly stand by when others are being harmed or find themselves in harmful situations? Overconcern for one's personal safety never has been and never will be an element in the happy church member's life. Self-sacrificial attitudes are the ones that lead to joy and happiness. Such was the case in Jesus's time, and such is still the case today.

One occurrence that held potential risk sticks in my mind. I was still in college, and one Saturday evening I left campus to drive to a church to see about a position as a summer youth director. Because of some commitments at school, I left later than I had planned. I knew I was low on gas but thought I had enough for the trip and did not take the time to fill up. Sure enough, about midnight, I ran out of gas two miles outside Tutwiler, Mississippi, in the midst of a rainstorm. Thankfully, a trucker stopped and gave me a lift to town. There I was, feeling as if I were in the middle of nowhere, wondering how on earth this could work out.

Soon the rain slacked up, and I saw a young couple coming out of a house trailer nearby. I knew nothing else to do but to walk up and introduce myself to these people. To my surprise, the man was a Methodist minister. He drove me around for thirty minutes, unsuccessfully looking for an open gas station. When none was found, he gave me the keys to his car and told me to use it to drive to my destination. I was so surprised! Here was a man who loaned his car to a total stranger and who stayed up to the wee hours of the morning when he needed to be fresh and alert to preach the next day. He truly had his loins girded and was ready for action at any moment.

What capped off the experience was when I returned, he had seen that my car had been filled with gas. Such generosity, trust, and hospitality made a tremendous impression on my young mind. The willingness to take personal risk for a rain-soaked college student was unplanned but very effective.

Not all encounters are as dramatic as helping a man beaten almost to death, but did not Jesus say that even a cup of cool water given in His name was significant? Some of the most impressionable occurrences from my childhood revolve around people seizing an opportunity for rather insignificant acts of kindness.

PROBLEMS WITH SPONTANEOUS SERVICE

Problem 2: Insignificance

One of these instances is still vivid now, decades later, and centers on the pastor's wife of a Church of Christ congregation that met next door to our house. One hot summer day, I had been playing with her son when she invited us to sit on her back porch to cool off. This was in the days when air conditioning was rare and ice water was the best choice to cool down. We sat down and soon the lady brought us not only ice water but also some cones filled high with vanilla ice cream. I could hardly believe my eyes! This was the first time in my life I had ever had an ice cream cone outside a drugstore counter. I thought such a treat was exceptional for a family to have, much less share with a neighbor's child.

To this day, I can still remember how special I felt because this lady gave a sweaty, little boy an ice cream cone on a hot summer day. Simple acts of spontaneous service, no matter how plain, go a long way toward filling the need we all have to be treated as special. Happy church members have a way of doing these small acts of kindness for each other.

PROBLEMS WITH SPONTANEOUS SERVICE

Problem 3: Busyness

Another problem keeping church members from spontaneous service is that of the general *busyness* on the part of so many in our society. We are constantly on the go. We have schedules to keep and deadlines to make. Those who do not are often looked on as irresponsible and lazy. At work are pressures of quotas, deadlines, and high expectations. Simply putting in a forty-hour work week is often not enough to meet the demands. At school, scholastic demands to excel as well as extracurricular activities gobble up huge chunks of time. Church activities are squeezed into whatever time is left—choir practice, small groups, mission trips, not to mention regular worship services. It is not at all unusual for families to go a whole week without everyone sitting down together to eat a meal. The children have to go here and there; Mom and Dad need to do this and that. Families meet each other coming and going on the street as everyone hurries to their activities or another important meeting. On top of all this, many live in a modified family structure: single, widowed, divorced, single parent, etc. The added responsibilities and issues in those families make a difficult situation even harder. Somewhere in all this, spontaneity falls to the wayside.

In Jesus's own life, much of His ministry to individuals was performed as He was headed to do something else. While Jesus was on the way to see about a synagogue official's daughter, He healed a woman with a hemorrhaging problem. As Jesus was going through Jericho on His way to Jerusalem, He healed a blind man. Even when He was on "vacation," He healed the Syro-Phoenician woman's daughter.

PROBLEMS WITH SPONTANEOUS SERVICE

Problem 4: Lack of Concern

Perhaps the biggest problem of all in preventing us from spontaneous service is a basic lack of concern. Christians can get caught up with the world's philosophy that a person needs to watch out for himself and his own alone. In spite of such teachings as the Golden Rule, many church members' life goals are hardly distinguishable from those of people in the world. Owning your own home, providing for your family, having a satisfying, good-paying job, and staying healthy are basics on many church member's lists. Strangely absent are items like sacrificially helping others, committing to serving the Lord, and generously helping those in need. Perhaps the reason many church members miss opportunities for spontaneous service is the same reason they miss any other opportunities: they lack real concern.

The story of the Good Samaritan from Luke 10 tells us about a priest and a Levite who both passed a beaten traveler. The reasons for their lack of compassion are not specifically stated. However, many people who are part of institutional services in their daily lives can easily fall victim to the idea that they have done their service on the job and should not be expected to be bothered by unexpected occurrences—even a beaten man on the side of the road. The hero of the story was an outcast, a Samaritan. He was the one who took the extra time and effort to help in a situation that he did not plan to encounter.

2

FIND YOUR NICHE

A happy church member has found her niche in the local body of Christ and is satisfied that her serving in that capacity is worthwhile. It is true that everyone needs to feel needed. This is especially true in church membership. For a Christian to be happy in her service, she must find a suitable, worthwhile task and be properly trained, even if she is gifted. She must then follow through by positioning that task as a high priority and doing it to the best of her ability.

What often happens, however, is that a member of the body does not feel included or accepted—not because of unfriendliness of the congregation but because she does not have a specific duty or task to fulfill within the structure of the church. People retreat from situations in which nothing is required of them. They gravitate toward situations in which they have a worthwhile role and are missed when absent. As long as there is a certain amount of recognition, appreciation, and satisfaction, they won't mind working and sacrificing. Nothing helps a member of the body feel part of the action like having her own responsibility.

PROBLEM 1: LACK OF SPECIFIC RESPONSIBILITIES

When a member of the body does not have a specific responsibility, she will often express her unhappiness in one of several ways. Perhaps the most common way is to become inactive and seldom attend worship services or any other church activities. Inactivity breeds more inactivity. Although the primary reason for church attendance should be one's faith and desire to worship and serve, group dynamics also play a large role. Church attendance involves interaction with others, and when people do not feel needed by those around them, few dig in deeper to find their place. On the other hand, when people have specific responsibilities, those responsibilities help give them a niche in the body of Christ. Feeling significant and needed gives them a felt need to attend church functions.

This principle was brought home very vividly one Sunday morning. As my wife, children, and I were driving to church, I noticed on the bank that it was negative nineteen degrees Fahrenheit. That was the coldest any of us had seen in four years of living above the Mason-Dixon Line. I tried to be positive but was pretty sure our church attendance that day might consist of only our family.

Shortly after I opened the church, to my amazement, up drove two members who lived farther away than anyone from the church. The streets were very slick since the salt could not melt the ice in such cold weather and their trip had taken much longer than the usual twenty minutes. But in they walked with smiles on their faces, ready to see what the Lord had in store for us that day.

Why did they put forth so much effort to attend? Many churches in the area had called off services, and no one would have expected them to make the hazardous trip. Yet they made the trip joyfully. The answer is that the husband had taken on the task of volunteer music leader. He had a responsibility that was his own and would not be done if he was not there. He had a specific role, and that gave him a good reason to attend.

There were many others who did not attend that day who lived much closer and were in good physical health. Although weather was the reason given for not coming, the root of their absence was a feeling of "Why bother?" They felt little of significance would be changed by their taking any extra effort to come, so they stayed home. When a member of the body has found her place of service and sees it as important, she will do almost anything to be there and, moreover, will be happier with her church and herself.

PROBLEM 2: UNTRAINED OR UNGIFTED

Other problems center around members of the body who have a specific task but who find themselves with responsibilities for which they have not been trained or gifted. Many in this category will simply stop doing what they have said they would do and then drop out of church altogether. When a person is incompetent for a task and, as a result, receives little gratification or praise, that task becomes very burdensome. Most members of the body do not want to cause a problem by being inept in their responsibility. So chronic absenteeism sets in.

Other members of the body react very differently to the problem of incompetence. These members, instead of dropping out, constantly point out what others are failing to do, hoping to cover their own inability or divert attention from their inaction. Although such behavior is often subconscious, it is quite destructive for the individual and church body as well.

PROBLEM 3: GUILT

A third reaction to being in a position outside one's abilities is that of guilt. When a person sees no fruits for her efforts, she begins to blame herself. Even though this person continues to work at her task and sometimes spends more time than is normally required, her efforts just do not bring the desired results. This person will often begin to feel self-doubt, discouragement, and guilt. In some cases, a member of the body will decide that she is not fit for any worthwhile task at the church. Obviously, this is not a satisfactory response and robs her of the ability to be happy about her church life.

Just as problems erupt when a member of the body is not functioning as God intended, some great benefits result when she does. One of those benefits is a healthy satisfaction on the part of the church member and church body as well.

When I looked around at my first congregation, there were so many jobs to be filled and so few members to fill them. Many of our members graciously accepted two, three, and even four responsibilities so that the organizational structure could be full and the work of the church could go on. It is only natural that in such circumstances a person will better enjoy some tasks over others. These tasks are probably nearer to what God intends for that person than the others.

One morning after Sunday school and before our worship service began, I watched a deacon welcoming *everyone* who came in, and he seemed to genuinely enjoy it. Visitors and members alike could sense his warmth, genuine concern, and exuberance. He was a natural at making people feel welcomed, needed, and worthwhile. It was evident he derived satisfaction from this role. He held several other positions in the church, and although many of those carried greater responsibility, none seemed to give him more satisfaction and enjoyment. In fact, from then on, I tried to make sure he was at the door greeting people every Sunday. What would be a burden to many people was to him an opportunity to serve in an area he believed God intended. Not only was he satisfied and happy, but his joy and happiness also affected the whole congregation.

In addition to satisfaction, there is also an increased willingness to serve when a person is functioning in the church body in an area to which she feels called and qualified. "I'll be glad to do it" are words that the average pastor and nominating committee hear too infrequently. When this response is given to a request for service, it usually comes from a member who feels she has found her place in the church body. She will have a sense of expectancy as she sets about the task. She feels that she has a vital contribution to make in this particular area and that she will fill it through the power of the Holy Spirit. Such a willingness to serve is infectious and can spread to other members of the body, leading them to examine their attitudes and motivation in church service.

Perhaps the most beneficial result of a member of the body finding her place in service is an increase in sacrifice for her Lord, her church, and other people. Just as at times in our physical bodies one organ will help an injured or inactive one, the same thing happens in a church body. Through proper service, a member is willing to sacrifice for the body (the church), its parts (other church members), and its head (the Lord). The extent of that sacrifice can be truly amazing and inspirational.

I was taught this principle at the first church I pastored. We had just completed the first building program and were seeing new faces at our services. One of those faces was Mrs. White, a retiree who still drove, took in sewing, kept her apartment as neat as a pin, and generally took care of herself remarkably well. This lady had been widowed when she was in her early twenties and never remarried. In spite of tough odds, she raised her son and provided for the two of them until he married and started his own family. Although she never had much of the world's possessions, Mrs. White had worked hard and made sure they had the necessities of life.

One day Mrs. White indicated she was interested in joining our fellowship. She had long ago given her heart and life to the Lord, and she already had a church home. However, our facilities were much closer to her apartment than her church's. She knew she could be more involved in church activities in a fellowship that met so close to where she lived. Mrs. White wanted me to know that there were many areas of service she would be unable to fill because of physical limitations, but she assured me she could pray and wanted to be a designated person of prayer for our church.

In the days to follow, I learned this was not an evasion of responsibility. She prayed for our church consistently and systematically. Every chance she had she was present in our worship services, doing the best she could at participating and making others feel welcomed. Regardless of whether she was able to come to the services or not, we knew she was praying.

As mentioned, during this time, we had moved into the church's first building. In one week's time, our church's budget increased by 40 percent because of the note on the building, utilities, insurance, etc. Although we were reaching new people, many were new Christians and just learning to tithe. On top of this, we had lost our biggest giving family. One Wednesday evening, our treasurer gave his report, pointing out that we were half a month behind in our finances. This might not seem much to many churches, but to our little congregation, it was enormous. We devoted the rest of our meeting that night to prayer about our debt.

A couple of days later, our treasurer came to me with an awkward look on his face. I had seen that look before when he seemed to be trying to figure out where this young, green pastor was leading the church next and how much would it cost. He was having trouble saying what he came to tell me, but he finally said, "We have had someone give us enough money to take care of our bills! But they want to remain anonymous."

Amazing! Fabulous! Here was one of the most striking answers to prayer I had ever seen. But who was the mystery person who had donated this gift? In retrospect, what happened next was almost eerie. I knew it was Mrs. White. No one even hinted at her being the giver, but I knew. She lived in a rundown apartment complex among transient tenants and drove an old car. Almost anyone else in the church could have afforded this gift more than her.

I jumped in the car and went to see her. At first, she tried to deny knowing anything about the gift. But when I started telling her I was going to return the money to her, she looked at me sternly and said, "That money was given to the Lord and His work. Don't rob me of the joy of giving to Him." Before it was all over, we both cried a little and laughed a lot.

After I left, I kept thinking of what a sacrificial gift this had been for Mrs. White. It represented a large part of her savings. She was willing to give it—in fact, *insisted* it be given—in a large part because of her identification and participation with the church. This had all grown out of her finding her role in the body of Christ and filling it.

Years ago, it was my honor to talk with a man who had done jail time and subsequently prison ministry for decades. He had been used by God to see people won to the Lord and even baptized into the body of a local church while they were still in jail. He literally saw the lives of prisoners turned from the gutter to God. This man of God had a stern warning for me about those who were won in prison and then released. He had observed that unless a releasee soon became realistically involved in a local church, he would inevitably fall back into his old friendships and old lifestyle. Just attending a church was not enough; he needed to participate.

To be genuinely happy, a member of the body needs to find an area of worthwhile service with which she is reasonably confident. Through such service, a church member can receive a tremendous amount of gratification that is unobtainable by any other means. This may require vigorous and soul-searching effort on the part of both the church member and those in charge of the task selection process in the church body. Such effort will be well worth the time for both the church and its individual members.

3

EVANGELISM AND OUTREACH

E vangelism is one area of church life that causes much fear, apprehension, and frustration. Strangely enough, it also brings much joy, exhilaration, and victory. For most members of the body, personal witnessing has become something that is either ignored completely or delegated to someone "more spiritual." Yet there is a level of joy and happiness a member of the body will never reach until he has begun openly sharing his most precious possession, Jesus Christ, with others outside the body of Christ.

There are several occasions in the New Testament when excitement, wonder, and joy followed the spreading of the Good News of Jesus Christ. One of the best examples is when Philip went to Samaria to share the gospel. The Jewish leaders in Jerusalem, including Saul, had begun openly persecuting the church after the stoning of Stephen. Many of the members of the Jerusalem church left town, like Philip, seeking to escape that persecution.

Strangely enough, Philip went to the city of Samaria, which was inhabited by a group of people who did not get along with the Jews. In spite of the persecution he had left and the potentially hostile crowd in Samaria, Philip began proclaiming the gospel. The results were astounding. Many of the Samaritans believed and miracles happened. Acts 8:8 tells us that, as a result, "there was great joy in that city."

Later, Philip was traveling down a road to Gaza where he met an Ethiopian. This man was studying the Old Testament scriptures as he rode in his chariot. He invited Philip aboard, and Philip was able to use those passages as he bore witness to truths of Jesus Christ. The Ethiopian was receptive and insisted that Philip baptize him right then on the side of the road. After they came up out of the water, Acts 8:39 tells us that the Ethiopian "went on his way rejoicing."

On another occasion, Barnabas was sent by the Jerusalem church to Antioch to check on rumors that Gentiles were being saved there. When he arrived, Barnabas found the rumors to be true; a large number of Gentiles had been converted and were gathering together. In this particular passage, it was not the one turning to the Lord who expressed joy over a conversion. Acts 11: 23 indicates that it was Barnabas, an observer, whose first reaction to seeing the new converts was rejoicing.

These are clearly examples of the joy and excitement that can result in not only a new convert but also in members of the body when they are witness to salvation. There are some exciting times awaiting those who will dare to go beyond the organizational, everyday routine of church life and share their faith in Christ.

One of the happiest times of my life took place as a result of an evangelistic encounter. Not far from our church building were some apartments that I frequently visited to invite people to church and to share the gospel when I could. I was given the name of a retired man who had just moved in. His wife of several years had just left him and his sons lived away, so this man lived by himself. When I made my first visit, I found a man trying to pick up the pieces of his life at an age when most people are ready to travel, enjoy their family, and take life at their own pace for a change.

We began chatting about the weather but then moved toward

spiritual things. I was surprised by this man's openness to the gospel. Here was a sixty-five-year-old with very little church background eager to hear the things of God. I had expected nothing but bitterness from him, but instead I found a brokenness that caught me unexpectedly. He joyfully accepted Jesus as his Savior.

He came to church and openly confessed his newfound faith in front of a bunch of folks he did not know. This faith invigorated his sagging ego and joy. It also boosted the happiness level of many of our church members. Several shared with me later how this man brought them great joy as they saw what the Lord had done in this stranger's life.

Perhaps the highlight of this experience came the night I baptized this new convert. It was January in Ohio, and after filling the baptistry, we learned the heater was not working properly. The water was ice cold. We brought in fifty gallons of hot water and added it to the baptistry, but it felt like we had done absolutely nothing to raise the temperature.

Right before the ceremony, I explained to the man our dilemma and told him we could wait until the heater was fixed and baptize him another time. But this new believer had waited long enough. Even if he turned blue with cold, he wanted to be baptized then. So we both waded down into the water and had a great time as this man followed the Lord's leadership in baptism.

After we had dried off and warmed up, it occurred to me how exciting it was to be a part of the whole experience. Such experiences only come when one is involved in sharing one's faith with others.

There have been numerous times when the excitement of being part of someone being born into the kingdom of God has warmed the heart of a church member like nothing else. I remember the excitement and joy of a lady just returning to the church building after her first time leading a person to the Lord and a young man talking about his experience in witnessing, wondering why he had not done it earlier. Having a role in someone coming to know Jesus

Christ as Lord and Savior is a uniquely joyful experience available to every believer.

OBSTACLES TO EVANGELISM

What is alarming, however, is that the majority of members of the body of Christ do not actively share their faith in Christ. Most will never know the joy of being a vital part in seeing a person turn his life over to the Lord. What happened since the time in Acts when it appears most believers were sharing their experience daily? The Bible is clear in Matthew 28:19–20 that it is the responsibility of believers to go to all the world and share the gospel. Yet even in the face of something as clear cut as the Great Commission, most church members still balk at evangelism.

SPECIALIZATION

One big reason for the lack of commitment to sharing the gospel is specialization, which is found in our working world. The day when a Benjamin Franklin could be outstanding as a politician, statesman, inventor, scientist, and writer is gone. Today almost every field has diverse areas of specialization. The medical profession's general practitioner has almost fallen by the wayside, with doctors specializing in oncology, pediatrics, neurology, radiology, and every other area associated with each part of the body. In fact, most specialized studies are broken down further into subspecialties. Those in the law profession have almost unlimited areas of specialization, with many never requiring a visit to a courtroom. Engineers can choose from electrical, civil, mechanical, and a host of other specialties.

All this specialization has proven to be very beneficial as our civilization has gained more knowledge and made advances in every area. The problem is that this mentality all too often is applied to evangelization. Whether admitted or not, many members of the body are content to let the well-trained clergy do the evangelism that is necessary for churches to grow.

There is a fatal flaw in this thinking, however. First, it is contrary to the biblical mandate from Matthew that all believers are to share the gospel. The Lord's work must be done the Lord's way. Second, no matter how gifted or skilled, professional clergy will never be able to reach and relate to every individual in a community. The church body as a whole must be involved.

ECLECTIC SPIRIT

Another reason for lack of involvement in evangelism by so many church members is the eclectic spirit that prevails in many church bodies today. This is the idea that if a person is genuine and committed in whatever he believes, then he is somehow going to be all right in the end. "Who are we to say that Christianity is the only way to reach God anyway?" If they are to be motivated to witness about Christ, church members need to believe that the lost person is eternally separated from God. There are too many interpersonal risks to take in evangelism if a person does not think the lost are really facing the wrath of God. What has subtly happened to many church members is that they have been convinced that God is too loving to send anyone to hell. If that were true, then it would eliminate the greatest motivation to take part in evangelism.

CHURCH LEADERSHIP

A third factor that has stopped church members from sharing their faith in Christ is church leadership. As strange as it may seem, there are church leaders who for one reason or another feel inept and thus unwilling to share their faith. Witnessing is definitely a skill that must be caught as well as taught. There is no better way to learn how to share the gospel than to see someone do it. Many church members have simply never seen any of their leadership share the gospel. Some members wonder how often the pastor actually does one-on-one witnessing himself. If the leadership has trouble in this area, then those who follow are not likely to go any further in their own witnessing.

As a young ministerial student, it was my privilege to serve as a summer youth director at Ingalls Avenue Baptist Church when Dr. Allen O. Webb was pastor. During those short months, I learned a great deal about pastoral evangelism. Still embedded in my mind today is the time Dr. Webb came to my office, asked me to stop whatever I was doing, and then asked me to go with him. A bit puzzled, I got in his car, and off we went to visit a family with an eleven-year-old boy who had never made a decision for the Lord. We arrived to find the boy and his mother at home.

After exchanging a few pleasantries, Dr. Webb got right to the point of our visit and shared the plan of salvation. There in his own living room with his mother watching, this young boy asked Christ into his heart. We were all overjoyed then, as well as the following Sunday when the boy made his decision public and was baptized.

I cannot remember what I was doing when Dr. Webb came to my office, but I know it seemed rather important at the time. In retrospect, I am sure there were some important things Dr. Webb could have been doing that day also. Yet he took time not only to witness to an eleven-year-old boy but to also help a young pastor-to-be see how it was done. People in the church knew Dr. Webb was always willing to share the gospel one-on-one and knew he was eager to show others how he did it. This made an impact on the attitude of the church members toward doing personal evangelism themselves.

FEAR

Of course, the greatest single factor that keeps members of the body from the joy of sharing their faith is plain and simple fear. There are fears about how witnessing will affect one's personal relationships. Others fear they won't know what to say or not say. Some apprehensions are based on a fear of rejection.

In a few cases, there may be reason to be afraid. I was visiting with a layman one day and, as we were getting out of his truck, a huge dog with eyes glaring and teeth bared rounded the corner of the house. We retreated back into the truck, deciding this dog was not going to allow for a teachable moment!

What is amazing is that so many have not realized that witnessing is like any other activity we do for the first time. A certain degree of fear and anxiety is to be expected. We all experience butterflies before a first date, the first time to speak in front of a room full of people, or at our first interview for a job. All normal people experience jitters before a new experience. Yet somehow Christians want to wait until they feel totally in control and at ease before they witness. It will never happen.

The Lord taught me about going ahead and witnessing in spite of misgivings years ago during the summer after my senior year in high school. There is one incident in particular that helped me see that fear is not a valid reason for not witnessing.

One evening I was headed home when I passed a man walking down the road. I had been hearing a lot from the pulpit about our individual responsibility to share the gospel with as many people as possible. Under conviction, with a good bit of fear, I turned the car around back to where the man was. As I neared the man and rolled down my window, I realized the man was very large—he looked like a giant to me. With a lump in my throat, I began witnessing to him. I no longer remember what I said, but to my amazement, this man stopped and listened to me for about fifteen minutes. In fact, right there under the stars, he asked Jesus into his heart and life. When he finished praying, he stood up with one of the biggest grins this side of heaven. The excitement in both of our hearts was overwhelming. The realization that such an encounter could make such a difference in a person's life was tremendously rewarding.

In the years since that experience, I still battle fears when I witness, and apparently I will until the day I die. Nevertheless, on that warm summer evening, the Lord displayed very clearly that He is big enough to handle any fearful situation if we will just trust Him.

LACK OF TRAINING

Over the years, I have held many training schools and sessions to help members of the body learn more about how to share their faith in Christ. One of the insights that I have had is simply that people have different personality types and, as a result, have different ways of relating to others, including how they share the gospel. There are those who are more comfortable with a structured, prepared approach in presenting the Good News. Others never seem to use these well but are good at a spontaneous approach, which incorporates the basics of the gospel. Others do well beginning with a structured approach to lead the conversation to spiritual matters but later use a more spontaneous approach as they grow in confidence.

READY FOR THE UNEXPECTED

A Christian needs to be ready for unexpected moments when someone is suddenly ready to respond to the gospel. Once I was wandering around in the back of our sanctuary between the time after Sunday school and before the worship service. At this church, it was like halftime at a football game. Everybody stretched their legs, took a break, and visited with others. In the midst of this, one of our youths walked up to me and said, "I'm ready to come forward; I just want to make sure when."

This young man had heard the gospel numerous times, but for whatever reason, that day he felt the conviction of the Holy Spirit. After going over with him a few things about salvation and then the details of how to make this public, it was time to start the worship phase. As John Bisagno once said, "If you want your preacher to get through on time, just let him know there is someone ready to publicly profess his faith in Jesus at the end of the sermon." That was the case that day. There have been fewer sermons during which it was so easy to get enthusiastic about preaching yet so easy to wrap it up.

ADDING NEW UNITS

It is appropriate for bearers of the Good News about Jesus to use the most effective methods available in carrying out our task. One time-honored method of reaching more people is not based on a new program of evangelism. It is not even based on a new way to teach small groups. This effective manner of reaching people is based on creating new units, whether that is in creating new Sunday school classes, starting new small groups, or even establishing a new church. This is not to say we need to stop growing the churches and units that are already in existence. What we need to determine is the manner in which we can reach the most folks. Many times this will be through new units.

The idea of starting new units has been around a long time. Part of the famous "Flake's Formula for Sunday School Growth" from over a hundred years ago is to add a new Sunday school class when the ones you have reach a certain size. Flake's method of growth by adding new units instead of just adding members to already existing ones has been proven over and over again. A class often feels comfortable with its steady number of people attending, even though there are many lost in the community. Class members do little visiting if they feel there might be a problem with space (physically and relationally) for visitors.

When a new class is formed, there is an inherent drive to fill the class and to get it functioning. Thus, outreach is magnified in a new unit. Small groups in any church will not grow in total membership very much without adding new units.

On the other hand, when new units *are* added, growth can be amazing. Briarwood Baptist Church in Dallas, Texas, led the Southern Baptist Convention two years in a row in average attendance increase for Sunday school. They were committed to adding a class whenever and wherever it was judged to be necessary. Classes met in theaters, country clubs, and other places miles away from the church facilities. This freedom not only enabled the Sunday school to grow but also the church to grow at a rapid pace.

The principle of adding new units certainly applies to starting new churches also. As part of the requirements for a college course, I had to write a paper related to sociological factors in religion. At first this seemed about as exciting as a beauty pageant for camels. I chose to study the growth patterns of Baptist churches in Jackson, Mississippi.

After pouring over three decades of growth, I was almost shocked at the results. The churches in the Jackson area had reached literally thousands of new church members, which of course led to a significant increase in the total number of members. The statistic that was most surprising was that the average number of members per church remained almost exactly constant—1,000 per church. That average membership never dropped below 950 nor rose above 1050 in a given year for thirty years. The overall growth in total members of the association occurred because several new churches were begun. When interviewed, sponsoring churches seemed to see an increase in the happiness level of their members. Overall, they were ecstatic about seeing thriving new churches they had helped start.

SPECIAL EVENTS

Many members of the body want to be a part of seeing people saved but just will never initiate witnessing conversations with others. These can be gently introduced to personal encounters through event-centered evangelism. These are events when the church has some activity to draw those outside the fellowship of the church to the church. Somewhere in the program, a clear presentation of the gospel is given.

In years past, lost people would be willing to visit a church during revival meetings. In fact, there are still areas of the country today where these are still viable. Our youngest daughter made her profession of faith at an area-wide crusade. Programs like Heaven's Gates and Hell's Flames and Judgment House have drawn hundreds of unreached and are still effective. Targeted events, such as a wild game supper and Super Bowl parties, blend entertainment with a gospel presentation. Ladies' gatherings of all types have had enormous success in presenting the gospel.

There are many ways to publicize such gatherings. By far the best way is still one-on-one invitations from church members going into the highways and hedges and bringing them in. In that situation, even though a church member does not specifically lead another to the Lord, when he is responsible for getting another person to a gospel event and that person responds, it is a joyous time all the way around.

When it comes to the happiness level of members of the body, seeing *new* members being added makes for an exciting atmosphere. All problems will not be eliminated by church growth, but it really helps to have the expectant feeling that comes with seeing the gospel received by many people as an outreach of the church. Christians who are part of a growing situation have more joy than those in a stagnant or declining church.

There is immeasurable excitement and joy awaiting those who are willing to overcome any obstacles in order to share the way of eternal salvation with another. In fact, to be a completely happy member of the body of Christ, it is essential.

4

FAMILY LIFE

One of the greatest challenges is how to handle all the problems we find in families, both in society in general as well as in our churches. Members of the body of Christ find they have matters that erupt in their families that take more than just an encouraging word to seriously affect any change. Reasonably happy, well-adjusted families seem to be the exception rather than the rule. Whether a church member is one who has a happy family life seriously affects how happy she will be in the body. To have a high level of happiness, she must take the principles of the Bible and seriously apply them to her own family.

This is not to say that when a member of the body of Christ is happy that she glides along with few family problems. Nor is it to say that her family life is immune to squabbles and disagreements. What it *does* say is that a key to one's happiness is directly related to how well a member of the body is able to learn and apply biblical principles about the family throughout her life.

No amount of church attendance, tithing, witnessing, or

other worthwhile endeavor can take the place of learning and applying scripture. Many church members have the erroneous belief that if they are faithful in one area of their lives then God will work out the problems in all the other areas. It is true that believers are assured that the Lord will provide physical necessities if they follow His instruction to "seek ye first the kingdom" (Matt. 6:33). This does not mean, however, that she can ignore her family in the name of serving Jesus and then expect a happy, contented family life.

Nor does it mean that because a person regularly tithes or teaches a class that God will whip her wayward son into shape if he was mentally and emotionally starved as a child. For a member of the body of Christ to experience happiness in her church life, she must follow biblical principles in the home. Following those principles in other areas but not at home will not ensure a happy home life or a joy in church membership.

The fact that a church member can follow certain biblical principles yet still have family problems is well documented in the Bible. The priest Eli was apparently a man of God, but he had considerable problems with his sons, at least partially because he did not discipline them properly. Samuel, who grew up in the environment of Eli's family, was strong in his fervor for the Lord but also had problems raising his own children. Isaac and Rebekah were both people of faith, yet their squabbles and deceit filtered right down to their children Jacob and Esau. Even David, as great a man of faith as he was, had significant problems with his own children after his sin with Bathsheba.

PRINCIPLE 1: LEAVE AND CLEAVE

What are some of these principles of family life that will lead to happiness? One is found as early as the second chapter of Genesis. In verse 24, God tells husbands to leave their fathers and mothers so they might cleave to their wives. Although this is not a command for spouses to disown or ignore their parents, clearly there should be a break from one's dependency on parents when marriage enters the picture. The "becoming one" between husband and wife mentioned in this passage really cannot occur until the emotional umbilical cord is severed.

Some members of the body have difficulty obtaining happiness because this severance has never been made. These church members may be some of the most faithful in attendance, they may work hard in teaching a Sunday school class, and they may have a big impact financially on the church through their sacrificial giving; but they are not truly happy. All the church work in the world will never make up for the fact that they have never truly left home. Overdependence on parents after marriage is hard to diagnose because there is a fine line between it and a healthy, genuine relationship. But when dependence is not controlled, unhappiness is the end result.

The happiest couples in the body of Christ have combined love and respect for their parents with bonding and autonomy with their spouses. Each married couple has separated enough from the others so the original family unit is no longer their primary source of security. When problems arise, they depend more on the Lord and on their spouse than on anyone else, including parents or children. This creates a sense of accomplishment, self-esteem, and confidence that enables each couple to be happier about themselves. When these couples attend church, their happiness shows and even spreads. Any problems that may arise in the body of Christ are not seen as insurmountable, because these happy couples have seen the Lord handle problems before.

PRINCIPLE 2: THE TEN COMMANDMENTS

Honor Your Parents

Several principles of family life are found in the Ten Commandments. The command to honor one's father and mother is one that has a remarkable impact on a person's life. The ability to grant honor and respect to those in authority has a direct effect on one's happiness level. When respect and honor for parents goes wrong, then the potential to be truly happy is lessened.

From the parents' perspective, Adam and Eve felt anything but happiness upon discovering that Cain had killed Abel. Eli's heart was heavy over the dishonorable actions of his sons. David was filled with remorse over Absalom's flagrant disobedience and attempt to take the throne.

From the child's perspective, Samson openly showed disrespect for his parents in his behavior and choice of a mate. That lack of respect eventually left him a sad, disheartened man.

Honor for parents is often tossed aside as no longer relevant or important. Tragically, this attitude has crept into our churches. Children of all ages who show little or no respect for their parents are too easily found on church membership rolls. Church members will never be fully happy while showing disrespect for their parents.

Respect for Authority

A side effect of the disregard of honoring parents is a lack of honor and respect for those in authority in the church. Certainly pastors, ministers, deacons, teachers, and others in areas of church leadership are no more perfect than parents. Yet the Bible calls us to grant authority to these people as they endeavor to fulfill the tasks of their positions. When that authority is not given, problems can arise, making the church body very unhappy. Members of the body who have difficulty getting along with church leaders often have problems with honor and respect at home.

When honor and respect are taught and given at home, the level of happiness is raised significantly. I recall one young lady who was happy with herself, others, and her church. She was a normal teenager who was learning about life, boys, and books with a positive attitude almost all the time. She enjoyed our youth group, and they enjoyed her. When work was needed, she cheerfully participated, and when it was time to play, she dove in.

One major element that separated her from others her age who were anything but positive was a respect and honor for her parents. Although her parents had their faults, she granted them the benefit of the doubt. This attitude carried over to church, where she treated those in authority with the same respect as her parents. Members of the body came to trust and rely on her, which led to even more joy in her life.

The direct result was a young lady who was happier with a better attitude than most of her peers because she followed her Lord's command to honor her father and mother.

Faithfulness

Another principle of family life found in the Ten Commandments is the prohibition of adultery. Infidelity in marriage seems to be more common than faithfulness. High percentages of both men and women admit to having at least one extramarital affair. When the numbers for sex outside marriage are considered, which includes those who are not married at all, the outlook is even grimmer. The majority of teenagers in this country have been involved sexually before they reach their twentieth birthday. These statistics are depressing, but what is even more discouraging is that these numbers have made deep inroads into our churches. Among church members, especially among those with nominal faithfulness, the statistics are no better than the general population.

As a result, guilt and remorse are commonplace. David's behavior of taking on sackcloth and ashes and refusing food after his adultery with Bathsheba showed the extent to which his soul was touched by his sin. Self-destructive behavior is not uncommon among a church member who is guilty of an adulterous relationship. Beyond that, the biblical account about David and Bathsheba implies that the reason the son born out of that relationship did not survive was at least partially because of David's sin. Church members who engage in adulterous relationships must not only deal with guilty feelings but also with a God who disciplines His own.

At this point, it should be pointed out that God's grace and mercy are certainly available to all members of the body who genuinely come to the Lord with a repentant heart. Adultery is not unforgiveable. Nevertheless, the results of such sin are often irreversible. In David's case, once he sinned with Bathsheba and she conceived, all the forgiveness in the world did not change the fact that she was going to bear a child, which led to David's decision to have her husband killed. Once the child died, even though David had been forgiven, there was no bringing the child back. Perhaps the most lasting effect was that David's children became uncontrollable after his sin. Before David's adultery, not one verse is recorded about any problems he had with his children. After his adultery and his attempt to cover it, we find one of his sons raping one of his daughters, one son killing another, and more than one son trying to unlawfully seize David's throne.

Although adultery can be fully forgiven in the eyes of God, its results can be devastating to the lives of those involved. Somehow the message has not properly gotten out, even in the church, that faithfulness in marriage is the best way to happiness in that relationship. Those members of the body who remain true to their spouses are among the happiest in the body of Christ. They feed their love and watch it grow, guarding it jealously and sometimes getting away so they can enjoy each other's presence. They do simple things to remind each other how special their relationship is. Happy members of the body have learned that fidelity to their spouse is important as is fidelity with the Lord.

Keep the Sabbath Holy

A third commandment that has an effect on the degree of happiness in a member of the body is the one related to keeping the Sabbath day holy. The Sabbath's primary purpose is to strengthen our relationship with the Lord, as well as our relationships with our family. Two extremes have developed among members of the body related to how the Sabbath impacts families. Each extreme has caused some to be less than happy. (For most believers, the Sabbath is celebrated on Sunday, so that is the term I will use.)

On one end of the two extremes are those who rarely spend time with their families on Sundays. If separated by distance, no calls or texts are sent. The concept of Sundays being a time for strengthening the family is totally foreign to these members of the body. Often Sundays are filled with activities centered at the church building, but which do nothing to promote family life.

On the other end of the two extremes are those who place family first and foremost at the expense of church attendance and involvement. This is far more prevalent in the body of Christ. Many church members come up with dozens of reasons they consider legitimate excuses for missing church, including activities such as going to the lake, going to see grandparents, attending sporting events, or just lazing around the house together. These people usually quote Jesus when He said, "The Sabbath was made for man, and not man for the Sabbath" (Mark 2:27). They rationalize any family activity that comes along, whether it interferes with worship or not.

The problem is that for a member of the body to be truly happy, her priorities must be in the proper order. When anything, even family, is placed before our relationship with the Lord, problems will eventually arise. Jesus spoke to this issue when He gave conditions for those following after Him. "If any man come to Me, and hate not his father, and mother, and wife, and children … he cannot be my disciple" (Luke 14:26).

Happy church members have learned to balance both worship and family time that are part of the Sabbath day teachings. They look forward to making contact with their spiritual family as well as their earthly family. Roots are firmly entrenched in both, and those roots should be nourished consistently. Truly happy members of the body of Christ know the joy and contentment of keeping both in perspective. As a result, they are better members of both.

Mutual Submission

One other major principle for a happy family life is taught in the New Testament in Ephesians 5:21. In this passage, mutual submission is commended as both the husband and wife should be "submitting yourselves one to another in the fear of God." Although this verse is not saying that husbands and wives have the same roles, it does emphasize that the husband should be subject to the needs of his wife and vice versa.

Couples have often come to my office with a list of problems a mile long, while *the* problem is that one or both are not actively seeking to care for the other's needs. My own marriage has suffered at times because I became too interested in making one more visit instead of seeing how my wife and children were doing. What would our church bodies look like if every time a wife had a need, her husband saw it as his God-called duty to be subject to her need? What if every time a husband was in need, his wife saw it as her responsibility to be subject to him? Married members of the body who have fully realized their happiness include the practice of this principle on a day-in, day-out basis.

Several years ago, there was a fellow who was not particularly happy with his church life, his family life, or life in general. He had a wife and two children, a good house, and a good job, but he was not very happy. Part of the problem seemed to be that he spent most of his spare time with his buddies, whether it was fishing, hunting, or participating in sports. These are not bad activities, but he was not spending much time with his wife or children.

Things came to a head one day and he just decided to leave the family. Thankfully, he got some wise counsel from a couple of his church buddies. He returned home and began spending more time with his family. There was not an overnight transformation, but day by day, his family relationships got better. His countenance improved, and he was obviously happier in both his family life and his church life. Whether he realized it or not, the improvement was a result of his application of biblical truths to his family life.

Crave for Attention

One area that has to be addressed in almost every extended family and church family as well is the small minority who will "holler wolf." There will be times family members and church members as well will be called upon to deal with situations in which someone needs attention and has learned to get it by having a problem. This situation is not an easy one to handle.

Members of the family and of the church family need to evaluate an individual's environment and personality and make an honest appraisal of how much help they can be when called. If a member is serious about helping others grow and mature in Christ, she will have to help some people realize that they can get attention in more constructive ways than through always having ill fortune.

There have been times when I received a frenzied phone call from a church member and knew not to rush right over because of my knowledge of the person and her circumstances. In these cases, ministry was best done in a slow, casual, confident manner showing the individual that she could be loved without having emergencies. This could lead to a higher level of happiness for her, her family, the congregation, and even me.

Every church with which I have been associated has had some

folks who were just not very happy. Invariably they had some pretty major issues at home. Sometimes these problems were not primarily the fault of the unhappy person, but the results were still not easily overcome.

It is obvious that over the years family issues in our society have increased to the point of being almost commonplace, but that does not mean the consequences are any less severe. The same could probably be said of cancer. Although better treatments are available today, the occurrence level seems high. The stress and impact of cancer are still huge to those who have it, no matter how common it is. This has an impact of the body of Christ as we live in the world.

We would be shocked if someone let go of an iron and the law of gravity did not take effect, pulling it down. We should not be surprised if, when a member of the body fails to follow biblical principles about family life, she ends up in a disastrous and unhappy situation. Certainly, we are all human and make mistakes, but we greatly improve our chances for a happy family life and happy church life when we adhere to the biblical guidelines for family life.

If we will look, there is much in the Bible to teach us about having a happy and fulfilling family life. This overall happiness will easily spread to one's church life and make for a better atmosphere in the congregation. After all, what is a good church but a church family where we are indeed brothers and sisters in Christ?

5

CELEBRATE

One of the biggest elements that characterizes a happy member of the body of Christ is that they have times of celebration and fellowship with the body. A sweet, sweet spirit is not just something they sing about, but they exemplify and express it with each other. In the context of a church body, there are hallelujah times that give opportunity to celebrate the joys and blessings of being a child of God. These are multiplied when they are shared with other members of the body. In fact, Christians who do not have an opportunity to share times of celebration with others are not as happy as they could be.

Such times of celebration should be a regular part of our worship times. There are times during worship that Christians need to be still and know God. There are also times when joy and celebration should be expressed in worship. There are frequent examples in Scripture of celebration within the context of worship in the temple. Expressing joy enhances a believer's worship experience and elevates his happiness level.

These times of celebration should go hand in hand with times of fellowship. Truly happy members of the body have casual times during which they simply enjoy each other's company. While times of worship are about getting to know God better, church bodies need times to get to know each other better as well. Those times can easily turn into great, old-fashioned, good fun that produces some of the happiest times for the members of the body.

OLD TESTAMENT PRECEDENTS

The precedents for times of celebration and fellowship are abundant in the Old Testament. Many times these two experiences are intertwined. When a church building is dedicated today, it usually involves a fairly big gala. Former pastors are invited, and preaching continues for most of an afternoon. Food is always part of the celebration, and there are congratulations for everyone.

When the builders had at last completed Solomon's temple in Jerusalem, they held one of the biggest dedication services in history. In 1 Kings 8, we read that the dedication for the temple was a worship service involving the sacrifice of 22,000 oxen and 120,000 sheep. In fact, "the brasen altar that was before the Lord was too little" (1 Kings 8:64) to hold all the offerings that were brought. Everyone in Israel was invited! Can you imagine inviting an entire country to a worship service?

The planning for the dedication called for everything to last a whole week. Things got rolling, and they extended the celebration an extra week, for a total of fourteen days. The people celebrated their Lord and fellowshipped with each other the entire time. "They went unto their tents joyful and glad of heart" (1 Kings 8:66).

Decades earlier, David was finally able to see the ark of the covenant brought to Jerusalem. There had been several obstacles to overcome including an aborted attempt resulting in the death of Uzza, who had touched the ark without permission. As the ark finally entered the city, King David's joy sprang out, and he actually began leaping about in the streets. The people gave offerings, and David took time to bless everyone. David distributed a loaf of bread, some meat, and a raisin cake to every man and woman (1 Chron. 16:3). Celebration, fellowship, and food were definitely the order of the day.

In the book of Psalms, where we get a good glimpse of what was said and done during worship in the temple, examples of celebration are quite evident. As the worshiper approached, he entered the temple with songs of thanksgiving, praise, and blessing to God (Ps. 100:2–4). The psalmist mentioned singing again in Psalm 95:1. "O come, let us sing unto the Lord." Other similar psalms clearly indicate the role that celebration had in temple worship.

A lesser-known passage that indicates the degree to which celebration and fellowship were emphasized in the Old Testament is Deuteronomy 14:24–27. This scripture deals with the situation of a follower of God who lived far from a place of worship. Travel often had to be on foot and made attendance difficult. An interesting alternative is given by the Lord to people who found themselves in extreme difficulty to giving their tithes.

In that day, tithes were often paid by bringing 10 percent of one's cattle, sheep, goats, and grain to a place of worship. The objects and animals making up the tithes would first be exchanged for money. Then the follower carried the money to "the place which the Lord thy God shall choose" (Deut. 14:25).

Notice the next step. "And thou shalt bestow that money for whatsoever thy soul lusteth after … and thou shalt eat there before the Lord thy God, and thou shalt rejoice" (Deut. 14:26). However, the next verse adds that any Levite who is around should also be invited to the party. Here is a passage that in essence commands the follower of God to spend his tithe, under certain circumstances, on a time of celebration and fellowship. Such a command should indicate the importance the Lord places on these activities even by members of the body today.

NEW TESTAMENT PRECEDENTS

In the New Testament also are passages that show that celebration and fellowship are a vital part of the Christian lifestyle. When the prodigal son returned home, the father's reply was "Bring forth the best robe, and put it on him; and put a ring on his hand, and shoes on his feet; and bring hither the fatted calf, and kill it; and let us eat and be merry" (Luke 15:22–23). In this story, the father represents God, and the prodigal son represents a sinner coming to obtain forgiveness and a right relationship with the Lord, which is a picture of what happens during a worship service.

When the son came home, a joyous banquet was thrown in his honor. Such should be the attitude and reaction among members of the body when a person comes to know the Lord's saving forgiveness. It is interesting that even though the father and son in this story were the ones primarily affected by what happened, everyone in the family, including servants, was invited to celebrate. Happy church members have learned the secret that it is perfectly acceptable to celebrate, rejoice, and fellowship over the victories and joys of other members of the body. Family members ought to help with each other's burdens, but just as important, they should celebrate each other's victories and joys.

In another parable (Matt. 22), Jesus compared the kingdom of God to a king who gave a wedding feast for his son. Extravagant preparations were made, and the king sent out servants to invite people to this feast. These invitations represent invitations to the kingdom of God. When Jesus chose a metaphor for the witnessing His disciples would do, He chose to depict it as someone inviting others to a time of great celebration and fellowship.

As the early church was being formed, the amount of celebration and fellowship taking place is very noteworthy. In Acts 2:43–47, we find these early church members were going daily to the temple. There was a sense of awe as many miracles were taking place. They often ate together, and some even sold their property and possessions to help others in need. Verse 46 tells us that the result of all this was "gladness and singleness of heart." Again, celebration and fellowship were key ingredients in the happiness of these followers of Christ.

FELLOWSHIP TODAY

Although church members need a vital fellowship life with other members of the body, a strong relationship with scores of people in a particular congregation is neither possible nor necessary. What *is* needed is a closeness with a few members who have similar backgrounds and outlooks. Smaller congregations usually do well in the fellowship area because they offer a manageable number of people to get to know and build relationships. Frequently, members of a small church have similar backgrounds and have common habits.

Although larger congregations have to work harder when promoting fellowship, they have the advantage of being able to break down small groups to very specific similarities. Whereas a small church may have only one or two classes for all adults, a larger church typically has classes for various adult age groups or interests, then further broken down into singles, couples, men, and women. Meaningful fellowship can be easily encouraged. Even though a member of the body may not know most of the people in the sanctuary on a given Sunday morning, he can have meaningful fellowship with the members of his small group. This allows people in a large church to still experience the happiness of a good fellowship.

CELEBRATION TODAY

Though a smaller church may have the edge with fellowship, a larger church body often has an advantage in the area of celebration during worship services. Large, talented choirs and praise teams, professional musicians, elaborate sound systems, and the electricity in the air when scores of voices join in worship can all make it easier to feel the presence of the Holy Spirit and contribute a magnificent celebration of God during a worship service.

Nonetheless, celebration can be part of worship even in the humblest of circumstances. My first pastorate was at a church that was meeting in the back of a savings and loan building when my wife and I arrived. All students, first through twelfth grade, met for Sunday school in a break room. The nursery was in the hallway. Everyone else met for Bible study in the "sanctuary"—a meeting room smaller than the size of a regular schoolroom. For worship services, our musical instrument was a two-octave air organ. Neither my wife nor I had ever worshipped in such an environment.

There was plenty of room for celebration in our new church, however. We majored on the Lord and His majesty. Testimonies and songs that magnified the Lord and His work in our lives helped to establish an air of celebration and expectation. Even though I was a new pastor learning as I preached, I tried to proclaim the power and faithfulness of the Lord and our need to simply have faith in Him. The electric air organ never sounded anything like the powerful organs I usually heard in churches, no matter how hard I prayed. Still, over the course of time, our services took on more and more of a celebratory atmosphere. This became a wonderful cycle. The more that atmosphere grew, the more celebration we had; the more celebration we had, the more church members invited and brought their friends; and the more new friends came and met the Lord, the more we had to celebrate!

For members of the body to reach their full happiness level, they must have a live relationship with others in the church body. They should long to be with each other, enjoying times of lighthearted fun and rejoicing over the joys of the faith. Every member of the body, no matter his age, needs time to simply enjoy his Lord and his brothers and sisters in Christ.

6

GRACE

J esus taught that our only hope for inheriting the kingdom of God comes through the grace of God. None of us deserve eternal life with the Lord, but we can have it because of the unmerited favor of God. When Jesus walked the earth, He exemplified this unbelievable grace. As He was dying on the cross and the guards were casting lots for His garments, Jesus said, "Father, forgive them; for they know not what they do" (Luke 23:34). Later Jesus directed His attention to one of the thieves dying on the cross and told him, "Verily I say unto thee, today shalt thou be with Me in Paradise" (Luke 24:43). This thief in no way deserved such a pardon, yet he received it because of Jesus's grace.

A LIFESTYLE OF GRACE

What is even more revolutionary about Jesus's teachings on grace is His emphasis on His disciples living a lifestyle of grace. He taught them that grace is not only something to receive but also something to be given to others. In Matthew 18:21 and following, Jesus exhorted His disciples to forgive others seventy times seventy. Then He told a parable to help them understand this teaching.

Jesus told about a king who brought in a servant who owed over $3 billion (10,000 talents) to the king. The servant obviously had no way to ever pay the debt, but the king had compassion on the servant and forgave his debt entirely. This forgiven servant later came across a fellow slave who owed the first servant about $6,000 (100 denarii). Although this was a substantial amount, it was infinitesimal compared the $3 billion from which the first servant had been given release. Instead of passing on the mercy he had received, the first slave had the second thrown into prison. Upon hearing about what the first servant had done, the king had this forgiven slave brought in. Angry at the injustice the servant had shown, the king had him delivered to the torturers.

To emphasize the point of the parable, Jesus told His disciples, "So likewise shall My heavenly Father do also unto you; if ye from your hearts forgive not everyone his brother their trespasses" (Matt. 18:35).

Jesus was emphatic that the grace God has given a believer should be passed on to those around him. Grace means that acceptance and value in the church body is not based on perfection. Nor is grace based on a member of the body's ability to live up to the standards of others. Happiness as a member of the body of Christ comes as a result of being simply accepted for who we are in Christ. The warm environment that is created when God's mercy is flowing from Christian to Christian is a dynamic factor in producing happy members of the body.

One afternoon as I was sitting in my office, a lady who had been visiting our church for a few weeks stopped in. She was distraught about something and began to share a tremendous burden that was on her heart. All I could do was listen as this young wife and mother poured out her soul.

When she was younger, she told me, she was reared going to

church and being taught about the Lord. Even though her family had its share of problems as she grew up, she knew that the Lord was the answer to all of them. When she got older and began to be more independent, she got involved with people and things that were less than godly. Still, she believed there was a better way with the Lord, even if she was not following it.

She met a young man, and they decided to be married. The wedding bliss soon wore off, however, and she noticed some of the same problems showing up in her new family that had been in her old one. One thing led to another and she had a child, not knowing for sure if her husband was the father. Grief and guilt had just about overwhelmed this lady. With tears in her eyes, she demanded to know, "Can Jesus forgive me?" One of the greatest joys of my ministry was to assure this lady that Jesus not only *could* forgive her, but it was what He wanted to do. I saw her turn her heart and life over to Jesus and watched the transformation of cleansing and hope He offered in her life.

When she could talk again, I asked her why she chose to bare her soul with someone she hardly knew. She said it was because she had found a place in our body of believers where she felt accepted. She had found a group of people who had shown her that whatever her problems or whatever her background, she had a place if she chose to take it. When a member of the body is willing to let Jesus's grace be hers, she will be much happier because she will experience the cleansing of being accepted for who she is.

BLOCKING GRACE

Tragically, the potential for joy and happiness is often spoiled because some members of the body have not allowed God's mercy to flow through them to others in the congregation. Whatever the reason for this, the results are often criticism, judgmental attitudes, lack of trust, and loss of happiness on the part of the members.

What is also tragic is that these attitudes are not new. They have been in the church almost as long as the church has existed. In Titus 1:12, a false prophet is reported to have stated, "Cretians are always liars, evil beasts, slow bellies." God's Word goes on to say that prophets who had such biased and negative opinions of others "deny Him [God], being abominable and disobedient, and unto every good work reprobate" (Titus 1:16).

Jesus taught that our ability to measure out grace to those around us affects our relationship with God. One of the parables that illustrates this is recorded in Luke 18:10–14. A Pharisee went to the temple, where he noticed a tax gatherer. Both the Pharisee and the tax gatherer were praying, although only one was justified before God—and that was the tax gatherer. Although he had much sin in his life, the tax gatherer came to the Lord with a repentant and humble heart. The Pharisee, on the other hand, had no use for the tax gatherer and showed him no grace. Even though the Pharisee had good deeds to his credit, his attitude kept him from being justified.

The power that members of the body have to bless each other by granting them grace or to harm them by not doing so was made clear to me several years ago in an unusual manner. The incident was between two brothers, but the principle can easily be applied to members of a church family.

I was completing a basic unit of clinical pastoral education one summer at a state mental institution. Since I both worked and lived on the hospital grounds, I often used my free time to participate in activities away from the institution. One weekend while playing tennis, my beeper went off, letting me know that some type of emergency had occurred at the hospital requiring the aid of a chaplain. My biggest concern at the time was wondering how long it would take to cool off and put on some appropriate clothes. Little did I realize what I was about to witness over the next twenty-four hours.

I checked in at the office and learned that a patient had died in the acute care unit. He had been a patient in the hospital for approximately twenty years. Walking over to the building, I began to wonder what the family would be like. Had his family kept in touch? Was he married? Did he have any children? What about parents or siblings?

Several things became apparent as the day wore on. For one thing, there would be few at the graveside service the next day. The family had had little contact in recent years with the man who died. Among those few who did occasionally visit was the patient's brother. He was a quiet man who bore a striking resemblance to the deceased and was apparently about the same age. At first glance, I presumed this was possibly the closest member of the family.

However, I was told a sad story about these two men. Several years earlier, these two brothers, who lived just down the road from each other, had gotten into a squabble. Words were exchanged, tempers flared, and the brother who was still living had told his brother he would never speak to him again. Being a man of his word, he held to it year after year. No matter what was done to try to work things out, there was no healing of the relationship. Eventually, the brother who had died, after being avoided for so long, snapped under the pressure and was admitted to the mental institution, where he spent the remainder of his life. As we stood by the grave, I thought with sadness of the results of grace not given.

Although this incident was between two genetically related family members, the same principle applies between Christian brothers and sisters. Members of the family of Christ may choose to not grant grace to fellow believers. The results, although not necessarily as dramatic as the example above, can be devastating to individuals and the local body as a whole.

STAFF/CONGREGATION RELATIONS

One specific area that needs to be explored under the topic of grace is that of staff/congregation relationships. There is an acute problem with too many congregations not granting grace to staff members and vice versa. There are literally thousands of ministers resigning churches each year with no other church to go to because of lack of grace being given by their congregations. Most ministers do not resign because of immorality, lack of spiritual insight, or even lack of work ethic. Usually, the reasons center around personality conflicts or quirks of character.

In New Testament church life, there was a time when Timothy apparently was having a problem in his ministry that was not based on anything over which he had any control. The church at Ephesus was giving Timothy some trouble because of his age. In 1 Timothy 4:12, Paul exhorted the young preacher to continue being an example of those who believe, whether there were members of the body who thought Timothy too young to pastor or not. Paul was not about to suggest the young man step down as pastor. Instead, he evidently felt it was the church's responsibility to change its mind about what they thought of Timothy.

There is no doubt the Bible lays down stringent guidelines to be followed in selecting and keeping pastoral staff. Too often, cultural and personal qualifications add or take away from these scriptural guidelines, with tragic results. Congregations need an attitude of grace toward those set apart for ministry. No one serves best in an atmosphere of judgmental attitudes, especially when those attitudes and judgments are based on something as arbitrary as an individual's personal opinion. Of all people, members of the body should realize that their leaders need to function in an atmosphere of grace.

My own home showed me the effect of grace on leaders. We had three daughters, and I took seriously the mandate to be a leader and example in everything from how to eat with mouths closed to conversing intelligently with adults. There were certainly times of failure in this role, especially when I lost my temper.

One especially difficult evening after punishing one of my daughters, it dawned on me what had really happened and that I had been unjust. One of the most difficult things I did was confess my fault to her and ask for forgiveness. It was such a tender, humbling moment when she looked up at me, gave me a hug, and simply said, "It's OK, Daddy." Such genuine, open grace makes it so much easier to be a motivated parent. Such grace makes it possible to be a better leader in church as well.

On the other hand, there are also times when a minister expects to be treated with grace by his congregation but has trouble dispensing grace. Some ministers think the members of the body should always give them the benefit of any doubt. Ministers can portray the attitude that war will be the inevitable result if their ideas and projects are not followed exactly the way they think they should be done. Any member of the body who does not cooperate can expect certain conflict. The example of Jesus's reaction to Peter after the resurrection gives us the example for minsters in giving grace even to members of the body who have failed or disappointed them. Peter's strong denial of knowing Christ did not prevent Jesus from granting him grace. As a result, Peter became one of the greatest leaders in church history.

Of course, specific sins and problems must be dealt with when they occur in any body of believers. In the case of the man openly living in an immoral relationship in the Corinthian church, Paul wrote that the church should remove him from among themselves (1 Cor. 5:13). But even in church discipline, grace must be exercised, as evident in what Paul told them in 2 Corinthians 2:6–7. "Sufficient to such a man is this punishment … so that … ye ought rather to forgive him and comfort him, lest perhaps such a one should be swallowed up with overmuch sorrow."

When grace is not applied, feelings are hurt, relationships are damaged, and doubts about God's control can arise. Nevertheless, when grace is given, members of the body get a glimpse of what heaven will be like, and the happiness level can soar!

7

FAITH

Members of the body who show deep happiness display a quality found in both Old Testament and New Testament biblical characters. In the context of this chapter, faith is an integral part in the life of the believer. It begins with trust in Jesus for eternal salvation and moves on to a deep, abiding commitment to rely on God for the needs of life.

Perhaps the prime example of faith in the Old Testament relates to Moses. God used him to lead the Hebrews out of slavery in Egypt and into the Promised Land. There were few prophets who did more than Moses to show the Hebrew nation how to exercise their faith. Miraculously, Moses, who was "slow of speech," spoke authoritatively and confronted Pharaoh, telling him of the coming plagues that God would send.

When the Hebrews left Egypt, Pharaoh sent an army after them. Moses was used to display God's power when the waters parted for the Hebrews to cross and then closed on the Egyptians after the Hebrews were safely on the other side. More miracles occurred as the children of Israel traveled through the wilderness. Obviously, not all the people internalized the faith of Moses, but Joshua and Caleb certainly did. And what a blessing they were for the nation after Moses's death!

Deep faith was mentioned by Jesus frequently and was often followed with joy and happiness. One such time was recorded in Matthew 9:20–22. A woman who had been suffering from a hemorrhage for twelve years was healed. Jesus told the woman, "Thy faith hath made thee whole." The joy of this woman's healing was precipitated by the exercising of her faith that Jesus could cure her.

Luke 7:1–18 chronicles a Roman centurion who had a slave who was sick and about to die. Hearing that Jesus was nearby, the centurion sent for Him to get His help. The centurion had great respect and compassion for this slave. Slavery does not normally breed joy or happiness. This time, however, gladness and delight were the result of the tremendous faith of the centurion.

Before Jesus reached the centurion's house, He was met by messengers from the centurion. They told Jesus that there was no need for Him to continue to the house. The centurion wanted Jesus to know that he believed Jesus could cure his slave by simply saying the word, that Jesus didn't have to be in the slave's presence to heal him. Jesus was touched by this faith, saying, "I have not found so great faith, no, not in Israel." Jesus healed the slave, bringing joy and happiness to both the slave and the centurion.

The key to the slave's healing and the certain rejoicing of the entire centurion's household was the faith displayed by this master for his slave. Striking in this incident is the ability to trust Jesus wholly and completely with the dire need of someone else. This Roman leader, though a Gentile, had learned what a difference faith can make when applied to life events.

Another example from the New Testament that helps describe the difference faith makes is the account of a father with a demon-possessed son (Mark 9:14–29). Few things in life can be as disheartening for a parent than to have a child with a disease that seeks to destroy that child. Surely this father had taken his son to every healer, physician, and priest possible, looking for a cure. For years, the son's convulsions had likely meant social isolation and abuse not only for the son but for the entire family as well. When the father heard of Jesus, off he went again in search of help.

The father found Jesus's disciples and told them of his son's problem. But his hope soon turned to despair when, instead of a miraculous cure, the disciples began arguing. By the time Jesus joined them, the father's thoughts of all his unsuccessful trips on behalf of his son had returned. Jesus chastised His disciples for their unbelief and then turned to this grief-stricken father and said a rather strange thing. "If thou canst believe, all things are possible to him that believeth" (Mark 9:23).

The father was overwhelmed. All his memories of past attempts to heal his son were blocking his way to belief. In a burst of honesty, the father called out to Jesus, "I believe; help Thou mine unbelief" (Mark 9:24). This was faith enough for Jesus, and the boy was cured.

What joy there was in that father's household that evening! The burdens and heartaches of a thousand nights were lifted. No longer would that son have to resign himself to a life with no friends, no wife, and no family. No longer would that father have to wake up in the morning with the pain of knowing his child was not right. No longer would that family have to bear the burden of being treated as unclean and separate. The open and honest faith of a remarkable father changed all that. Happiness took on a new meaning on that day for this family.

One other remarkable illustration of faith in the New Testament occurred when Jesus sent out his disciples in groups of two (Mark 6:8–12). The instructions surrounding His commission to go are extremely noteworthy. He told the disciples not to take bread, money, or bag, and they were limited to one tunic. Why was Jesus limiting their supplies? Wouldn't they balk or even bolt?

By this time, the disciples had seen how Jesus's faith had prevailed time and time again. It was His desire to not only display faith to His followers but also to pass it on to others and encourage them to use their faith. He especially wanted His inner twelve disciples to build their faith. So they all went out with little more than faith, but it was enough. They returned full of excitement at what they experienced.

At times, a Christian's joy and happiness is hampered because he is not exercising faith as he encounters the daily occurrences, trials, and needs of life. Too often, a strong daily faith is looked upon as an option, even by committed members of the body of Christ. Only when a person is using his faith to handle the daily needs and events in his life will he reach his full potential of happiness.

PRINCIPLES REQUIRING FAITH

Relational Principles

Relationally, many church members are not happy in their relationships with other members of the body. They have not taken the steps of faith necessary to incorporate Jesus's relational principles into their lives. Jesus gave some powerful commands in the area of how people should relate to each other. These commands take faith to follow. It is not easy or natural to love your enemy or turn the other cheek. Going the second mile is not intrinsic to human nature. Yet church members who do not faithfully live by these precepts are lacking the joy of relational warmth.

The only reason to not follow these teachings of Jesus is simply that they make little sense to some. Human nature tells us that happiness is found by preserving and protecting our own things and character. Even within the body of Christ, it is not uncommon to find those who are holding grudges, displaying aggressive anger toward others, or holding back offering sacrificial help on behalf of fellow members. Sadly, thousands of new congregations have been formed not by a desire to grow the body of Christ but because one group could no longer get along with another one inside the confines of a church congregation.

Dr. Jim Futral, past executive director of the Mississippi Baptist Convention, tells the story of a church that realized they were outgrowing their current building and decided to construct a new building. A committee was formed, of course, and they were making progress toward their goal until the decision for what brick should be used on the exterior. One group in the church felt strongly that a traditional red brick was the only answer. The building committee recommended a tan brick. Eventually, the red brick group saw they were not going to get their way. So they did the only honest thing they thought they could do: pull out and start a new church. In the meantime, the established congregation went on and built a beautiful, tan-bricked building.

As time went on, the red brick group found a house to purchase to use as their worship center. They began to grow and one day decided it was time to build a regular church building. A committee was formed, of course, and progress on the plan went along fine. Of course, they too had to make a decision about what brick to use. One would think there would be no question about what to use. It would be red brick, right?

No, over the years, the red brick group had noticed that the tan brick used on the other building was actually quite attractive. In fact, the red brick people decided that instead of traditional red brick, they would use tan brick also. Today, there are two tan brick church buildings just down the road from each other. It is true that the Lord has used such disagreements to plant new churches. But it remains that church members will not be happy with other members of the body when biblical precepts of faith are not followed.

The church body experiences great joy and happiness when members step out by faith in the areas of Jesus's relational commands. To see someone have the weight of the world lifted because he followed Jesus's command to ask forgiveness from one he had wronged is a joy. To see the tears of parents when their teenagers let them know they love them is heartwarming. To see people who have not spoken in years restore their relationship often leads to revival within the body. These warm relationships can only be fully experienced by members of the body who are willing to walk by faith to follow Jesus's precepts.

Financial Principle

Many members of the body enjoy the comfort of believing that the Lord will provide for their financial needs. To be justified in anticipating comfort in this area, we need to be acting out our faith. When the prophet speaks of the Lord pouring out blessings in Malachi 3:10, the condition for those blessings is that followers bring the whole tithe to the storehouse. In the New Testament, when Jesus exhorts His disciples not to be anxious about the things they need, He assures them those needs will be supplied if they put the His kingdom first in their lives.

Financial worry is one of the biggest concerns people have and it is also seen among church members. Those who are happy and confident that the Lord will provide have derived this assurance because of their expressions of faith in the past. Those who have not been faithful in their financial commitment to the Lord often find little comfort when they seek His help in times of financial crises. On the other hand, those who consistently place the Lord's work first, both financially and otherwise, have a deep-seated confidence and peace when they face seasons of financial uncertainty that afflict us all at times.

In one church I pastored, our body of believers saw the joy that faith-directed giving can bring. Our sanctuary was too small to accommodate the numbers that were joining our fellowship. There was more than one time when a family would walk in the back door and then turn around to leave because there was no place for them to sit.

Faithfully, the building committee went through the process of getting plans for a new, spacious sanctuary and began getting bids for construction. When all of these were too high, one member of the committee, who was a master carpenter, stepped forward and said he would volunteer his services to supervise the construction. Another who knew concrete construction said he would contribute his time to work the slab and parking lot. Both of these sacrifices saved the church hundreds of thousands of dollars.

This got the cost of construction down, obviously, but the committee had to take the project to the church body for them to vote. The cost was still going to be enormous for this congregation. So we began a pledge campaign to pay the debt, or at least put a dent in it, over a three-year period. We saw strong participation by most of the congregation, regardless of financial wealth or lack thereof.

An amazing thing happened on the second anniversary of worshipping in the new building. We burned the note and celebrated being debt free. We saw so many members excited and happy about their giving, which had been totally based on faith. The money they gave did not cause them disappointment because they did not have as much for themselves as they could have; their generosity gave them great joy. We celebrated because we were reaching more people than could have ever been possible with our smaller sanctuary. Those who gave so generously could legitimately consider themselves as part of the conversions and baptisms because of their faith-giving to see the larger place of worship erected.

Bible Study and Prayer

Mentally, many church members have a hard time dealing with the circumstances of life. We can all use help in coping with day-to-day occurrences. People of faith can express that faith by taking time to develop the discipline of a personal, daily Bible study and prayer time. It is surprising how many church members want all the comfort, help, and security the Lord has to offer but never display enough faith to search out God's Word or communicate with Him through prayer.

One Sunday morning, we had a particularly moving worship

time. The father of a family who had been coming to church for a while had accepted the Lord that morning. It was exciting to see this man join with his family in a commitment to live in a new way of life.

The next week, I dropped by to see this man and to pray with him. At that time, as was customary, I gave him a copy of a personal discipleship book and encouraged him to start attending a weekly class for new church members studying this book. Unexpectedly, he told me that he and God had their own thing going and they could handle things just fine without any extra help.

Needless to say, when I returned to check on him a few weeks later, things were not so fine. The specifics of the problems boiled down to something, surprisingly enough, that he would have learned if he had been in our discipleship study that week. After we had talked and I had told him about what we had studied, he looked at me and said, "You know, I guess there is something to studying what the Bible says after all!" Those members of the body who have the faith to make the time to read God's Word and communicate with Him seem to handle day-to-day crises of life much better than those who do not. Those who neglect this element of faith are often puzzled when the sense of victory is absent.

A good biblical example of using faith in handling the problems of life is found in 1 Samuel 30. David and his men returned to Ziklag, their home, to find the Amalekites had raided the city. They had burned the houses and carried off the inhabitants, including David's two wives. To add to David's personal distress, his own people began speaking of stoning him because of their bitterness at losing their families. Here we see social, financial, and mental pressure all rolled into one.

In the face of this tremendous pressure, David "encouraged himself in the Lord his God" (1 Sam. 30:6). By exercising his faith in this situation, David was not only able to track down the Amalekites, but he was also able to recover what they had taken. The rejoicing and relief that followed were a result of what happens when one exercises faith in the midst of life's problems and difficulties. Of course, David not only *knew* scripture; he was inspired to write part of it.

PERSISTENCE IN FAITH

A member of the body of Christ may have used his faith time and time again to see God work. But at some point, he may feel tired and want to simply coast along and rest for a while. The problem is that life never coasts along. There are always areas of life that benefit from an expression of faith. Faith is not a drudgery that tires us out; it is an uplifting boost that Jesus spent much of His ministry encouraging us to live out in our lives.

Caleb is a striking hero in the Old Testament. When he was young, he and Joshua stood up to ten other Hebrew men and encouraged the children of Israel to conquer the Promised Land. Caleb understood that the inhabitants of that land were strong and well-fortified, but he had a firm faith in the Lord's promises. In the midst of ridicule and criticism, Caleb stuck to his beliefs.

The wandering Hebrews sided with the ten other spies and did not attempt to conquer the land the Lord had promised them. Nevertheless, Caleb held on to his faith and had remained faithful when almost forty years later Joshua led the Israelites into Canaan. In fact, when Caleb was eighty-five years old, he approached Joshua and asked for the land promised him by the Lord in those earlier years. This portion of land had not yet been conquered and would require faith to take over. Caleb was still seeing the world through eyes of faith and was successful in conquering and then living in this land.

Other instances of men and women living by faith no matter what their age can be found throughout the Bible. Never is there an instance where the Lord excused someone from a daily walk of faith simply because the person was old or tired. Unfortunately, there are members of the body of Christ who are missing out on happiness because they think they have used their quota of faith, that it is someone else's turn to carry the banner. These people have talked themselves out of faith, service, and ultimately, happiness.

HOLDING ON TO WHAT THEY HAVE

Some people do not apply their faith because they are content to stay with the church's status quo. They are trying to hold on to the way things currently exist. Whether a church body is trying to reach new members or to build a new building to accommodate the numbers visiting, people who are content with where the church is have trouble trusting the Lord to work out the inevitable complications that come with church growth. New faces have new problems, and they have new ideas! Having more people means there will need to be an expansion of organizational structures. Having new facilities means there are more financial obligations and potentially the need for more staff, which means a bigger budget.

Too often people content with the status quo will say things like "We have a good fellowship here. Let's don't mess it up by bringing in too many people too fast." Or they may say something like "We're comfortable with the folks in our class. Why should we restructure just to get ready for some people we don't even know?"

Jesus gave an important mandate to the church to reach out beyond its walls and bring others in. This mandate required change and faith. To incorporate new faces on a consistent basis into its life and ministry is not an easy thing for a body of believers. In fact, it takes a great expression of faith. But in the midst of the challenges and uncertainty of church growth, there is a happiness that is really inexplicable. Members of the body can have joy when their church family consistently brings in new members. In that church body, there is an exhilarating atmosphere of expectancy and excitement, not unlike what is found when there is the birth of a new baby in a family.

COMFORT AND SUPPORT

One of the functions of the body of Christ is to supply a network of comfort and support for its individual members. Such a network is an invaluable tool for ministering during times of illness, death, or other crises. This network becomes imperative when family supports are crumbling or are far away during those times. Most churches understand this. The early church certainly did.

At the same time, what is also needed is the support God gives His children when they show faith in Him. In Romans 1:17, Paul simply and plainly encouraged the church in Rome to live by faith. Paul knew firsthand that the happiness level for members of the body could not be all it could be unless they lived by faith.

One of the best examples of seeing God work to bring happiness to people of God who exhibit faith happened in the life of a pastor friend of mine. Both of our churches were in a building program while we pastored in the same area. Every once in a while, we would get together and share how God was helping us solve what seemed to be impossible problems related to the building. For example, many times financial problems were not solved by the traditional way of people giving more money. God often had better ways of blessing us.

One problem that my friend faced was getting the excavation done before the construction could begin. The best bid they had found for the excavation was strong into five figures. There was no way the church could pay that amount and still have enough to start building. The congregation prayed and prayed, asking the Lord for a way to solve their problem.

One Wednesday evening on his way to church, the pastor saw a man working a bulldozer in a field. The pastor felt led to stop his car, risk being late and dirty for church, and plod out to talk to the man. The pastor learned that the man was the owner of the bulldozer as well as some other nearby equipment. He asked the man what he would charge to level the church's property. After thinking a minute, the man said, "You're just down the road, right? My equipment is already right here. How about $5,000?"

This put the church back in business! Even more, it instilled in that body of Christ a tremendous happiness that the Lord was still at work in their midst. Faith that is exercised in our daily lives has a way of allowing us to develop an assurance in the midst of life's storms.

8

STEWARDSHIP

One area of a believer's life that can bring a huge amount of joy is that of stewardship. When members of the body of Christ follow Jesus's instruction about giving out of love as well as commitment, then they will reach new heights of elation and joy. Perhaps this is because true joy comes more through sacrifice than circumstances. The teaching that "it is more blessed to give than to receive" (Acts 20:35) is a major cornerstone in the life of the truly happy church member.

Yet there are problems that can stand in the way of a member of the body knowing the joys of stewardship. In fact, financial and material stewardship is one of the biggest areas of the believer's life in which misgivings, misunderstanding, and just plain fear run rampant. Some people moan when they know the sermon will be about stewardship. Unbelievably, some actually leave when they find out the sermon is about giving. Others subtly ask how long a series on money is going to last. Because of this, there are some pastors who preach the Word vigorously and with passion yet *never* preach a sermon on tithing. One pastor has a visiting preacher to his church every so often to preach on stewardship, but he never addresses the topic himself.

CLERGY AND LAITY GIVING

What is at the root of such widespread fear and misunderstanding on the part of pastors and laypeople alike? With pastors, it is sometimes due to forgetting what the purpose of tithing and giving is. They start to think that when they preach on giving and issue a call to the church to be faithful and consistent givers, it is like they are asking for more money for themselves. After all, in most congregations, a large percentage of what is collected goes toward staff salaries. But what the pastor has forgotten is that people are not giving to the pastor. They are giving to the Lord.

In the Old Testament, much of what was given went to support the temple priests—probably even a higher percentage than supports current-day church staffs. Still, throughout Scripture, the predominant thought is that these gifts are for the Lord. Such verses as Malachi 3:10 include phrases that the Lord speaks, such as "that there may be meat in Mine house" and "prove Me now herewith." These clearly show that God Himself sees the tithes brought to the temple as His own. In the day-to-day schedule of church business, this truth can be forgotten even by God's anointed leaders. When this happens, the results often lead to an unhappy church leadership.

A church needs financial resources to reach its fullest potential in ministry. To make sure these resources are available to the church, the members of the body must be taught and challenged from the pulpit. It is foolhardy to expect to just pray a lost person into relationship with Christ without taking any opportunity to share with the lost about knowing Jesus as Savior. Equally as foolhardy is the pastor who prays for his church to give the funds for all the needed ministries without sharing with the members the biblical principles of how and why a believer should give to the Lord's work. Frustration is the inevitable outcome.

Conversely, there is joy for a pastor who consistently teaches and preaches sacrificial Christian stewardship. Principles of Christian giving, such as the fact that everything one owns is really entrusted to him by the Lord, add a different perspective to the mindset found in the world. When a pastor teaches these principles in a clear, concise, and consistent manner, he is strengthened. He is reminded that he is doing more than raising money to keep an institution's doors open; he is challenging members of the body to be proper stewards of God's possessions.

Another positive effect when stewardship is taught is that members of the body will get a feel for what good Christian stewardship is all about. When this happens, the church body is edified and the task of the pastor is more of a joy.

The problem with laity and giving is similar to how some pastors struggle. Some members have a faulty perspective about why they are giving. Most are willing to sacrifice dearly to give to those they love and with whom they identify. It is not unusual for parents to provide their children with televisions, telephones, computers, cars, and thousands of dollars of other valuable and expensive "necessities." Sadly, these same parents may offer their Heavenly Father a token amount each month. Why would someone who identifies as a child of God be willing to sacrifice so greatly for her family but so little for her Father?

It goes back to not understanding that when we give to the church, we are giving to the One who loved us enough to send His Son to save us and to bring us into eternal life with Him. Some think only in terms of what the church needs and not at all of the effect giving has on their happiness. In fact, many of those who occasionally put a little in the offering plate begrudge what they do give. All they see are other things for which they could use that money. Unhappy givers easily become unhappy church members because they do not recognize the object of their gifts.

On the other hand, when a member of the body begins to catch a vision of what true godly giving is all about, the results can be astounding, even to her. The joy and happiness that result are a sizable encouragement not only for the individual member who follows Jesus's teachings on giving but also for the body as a whole. Instead of giving resentfully, they give abundantly and sacrificially with a joyful heart.

While visiting a fellow pastor, I asked him the standard question of how things were going at church. "Great!" he replied. "We're having a stewardship revival, and our folks are really receiving a blessing." I had never heard of such a thing and asked who was preaching. He told me a name that was not familiar to me and then added, "He's a layman who has just been turned on to God's principles about giving." Sure enough, this church not only began to see its giving increase, but the members became more joyous and happier. Just as the joy of salvation is open to every believer, so is the joy of Christian stewardship open to every sacrificial giver.

IDENTIFICATION WITH YOUR CHURCH

Members of the body should also be aware of the principle of identification with their own body of believers. But there are pitfalls to happiness if this is taken to one of two extremes.

On the one hand, there is the church member who strongly identifies with the church to which she gives. On the surface, she appears to have a healthy and happy view of giving. But she can so identify with her church that she feels she has earned the right to voice her opinion every time money is spent, especially if it is in a manner different from her own point of view. Monetary decisions are constantly made in churches, and they rarely satisfy every member. One who overidentifies will usually make a big issue of each such expenditure. Arguments over colors of brick, position of instruments on the stage, and even how much to spend on paper towels occur because individuals feel they have given enough that they should be making all those decisions or because it is "their" church and they want to have a say in every single decision.

Such behavior leads to unhappiness not only for the member who is overidentifying but also for others in the church body. The congregation as a whole may simply bow to the requests of this one person in the interest of peace within the body. Of course, this stifles the body, and no one is happy. The opposite reaction is that the congregation goes with the majority opinion and the over identifier gets her feelings hurt and leaves the church. Neither of these reactions makes for happy church members.

Of course, the opposite is the under identifier. This person has no idea where the money she gives goes. This is not a person who completely trusts the church officials to make wise and holy judgments with the church's money. This is a person who only attends a few Sunday morning services and simply does not identify with the body. Her friends are not primarily in the congregation of the church she attends. The under identifier has interests that lie predominantly outside the boundaries of what is happening within the body of believers where she worships. There is little joy in her giving because she is not really interested in what happens to what she gives and gives more out of obligation than because she is a part of something that is changing the world. She gains little happiness from her church life. To an extent, she also robs joy from others in her church body because her church will never be all it could be apart from her participation.

A member of the body of Christ needs to balance her attitude between concern about how the money she gives is spent and trust that God will guide those making decisions about how the church should use the money she gives. Even in the body of Christ people make mistakes, but a happy church member believes that the Lord is in control and will bring about what He determines. The body of Christ should make proper and wise business decisions, but each member needs to learn to trust that God is in control of all matters in the life of the body, including finances. As one man told me, "Preacher, I feel good about my giving here. Not just because I trust you and the staff, but because I trust God."

WAITING ON CIRCUMSTANCES

Every congregation has people who do not give, or who say they would give more if things were different in their lives. This member would say if only she did not have this bill or that financial burden, she would be more than willing and able to give. Coupled with our society's view of so many "necessities," she thinks surely God understands and makes allowances for her lack of giving. Actually, I believe God understands perfectly and judges lack of commitment accordingly.

No one can have this attitude for an extended period and remain happy with her relationship with the Lord and His church. She will begin to lose the joy she derives from what God is doing through her church. Happiness often comes when those with whom we are involved succeed or are victorious in their lives. When we are involved in our church through consistent, sacrificial, and proportionate giving, we are more joyful when we see lives changed and spiritual victories within the body. When someone comes to know the Lord through a body of believers, she reaches that decision to some degree because of every faithful giver. Each one giving has indirectly supported the staff who likely had some role in this person's decision. Sunday school literature, which possibly influenced this new believer, was purchased as a result of the giving of faithful members. The facility itself where this new believer will grow in her Christian walk was made possible through the giving of members. Because of these influences, every faithful giver has a legitimate right to shout with joy when a life-changing decision is made in her body of believers.

So what about the person who has rationalized her way out of giving? She who has an insignificant role in bringing something about has little joy when it is accomplished. All the self-induced hype in the world will not substitute for the true joy of knowing we are a large part of something important. The church member who has excused herself from vital giving eventually excuses herself from vital joy.

CONSISTENT GIVING

The Scriptures entreat members of the body to be consistent givers. When Paul called on the Corinthian church to take up a collection for the church in Jerusalem, he specifically told them to take a collection the first day of each week. One reason for this was certainly the amount that could be raised through such a method. Paul knew that the common people in Corinth had little money and a one-time collection would do little to alleviate the problems of the Jerusalem church. However, by consistently having the believers in Corinth give over an extended period of time, the gifts would accumulate and become a considerable amount.

I am reminded of this every year while getting my income tax forms prepared. There is little about the whole procedure that is enjoyable, but there is this one bright spot. Each year we get a form from our church showing what we gave during the past year. The amount often leads me to praise the Lord while filling out those IRS forms! Any member of the body who consistently and systematically gives to the Lord's work has probably experienced this happy surprise. I know that the money we have contributed has gone to building up the kingdom of God in foreign countries, has supported children's homes, has sent missionaries out, has opened seminaries, and has impacted hundreds of other ministries.

Consistent giving causes our actions to affect our feelings. Every believer has times in her life when circumstances are not all that they could be. Everyone experiences disappointments and setbacks that affect her feelings. One way to counteract this is positive action. By repeating positive behavior, even when she does not feel like it, she can lift her feelings. One positive action that can help pull a believer out of the dumps is to give habitually. Members of the body who consistently give sacrificially to the Lord seem to handle depression better when it comes. Repeated giving affects our feelings.

EYESIGHT

Most problems the average church member has with stewardship come from either having her eyes on what she has or on what she does not have. She can get so caught up with what she already owns that she spends most of her time and energy just trying to hang on to it. The iconic example of this is from Luke 12, the parable Jesus used about the rich man and his barns. When this man had a bumper crop, his main concern was how to hang on to every bit of it rather than thinking about how the excess could best be used for God's service. The man's excitement over his abundance was very short-lived. He died, leaving everything behind.

A believer may, on the other hand, focus on what she does *not* have. She thinks if she can ever get a new car, some better furniture, or that dream house, she will have all that she needs and then she can give to God. As a child, I remember really wanting a certain new bike with lots of chrome. I thought if I could ever get a bike like that, then I would be satisfied for years. What else could I possibly need? I did get that bike, and I found that within a couple of weeks, I was yearning for something else. There is always the next plateau of economic success just beyond where we are. If economic success is the goal, it is tempting to rationalize not tithing or giving to the Lord's work. When a member of the body of Christ puts her eyes on what she has or does not have, she is not happy. On the other hand, when she is totally committed to giving whatever the Lord asks of her, she will experience mirth, spontaneity, and happiness.

In 1 Chronicles 29, David and his captains gave a remarkable quantity of gold along with impressive amounts of silver and precious gems, and their generous giving caused them to greatly rejoice. When Moses led the children of Israel to give an offering to build the tabernacle, the people got so enthused with the spirit of giving that Moses had to command them to stop because they had given more than enough.

In the New Testament, Paul took up a collection for the impoverished Jerusalem believers from the Macedonian church, who were themselves in poverty. Still, they gave liberally, even "beyond their power" (2 Cor. 8:3). The result was an abundance of joy among the Macedonian believers.

Members of the body who are happy have learned that one of the secrets is to be simply a good steward of God's possessions. Everything we own belongs to the Lord; we are His stewards over His possessions. When we handle the Lord's possessions as He would have us do, we experience freedom and joy. Rather than being burdened by our financial obligations, we rest in the knowledge that God can handle anything so He can certainly handle our finances and possessions. Knowing this frees us to watch God work.

I learned much about this principle in my first pastorate, fresh out of seminary. My wife and I felt the Lord leading us to a small church in northeastern Ohio. Although the church had previously only had part-time pastors, I felt for this particular church to become all God intended, I needed to spend full time as pastor. The small congregation agreed and doubled what the previous pastor had been paid. Even at that, my salary was less than minimum wage. My wife got a job as a secretary for an insurance agency, making more than I made.

It soon became apparent that we would not be able to make ends meet with just these two small salaries. It became very tempting to focus on all the things we did not have. There were times of doubt, uncertainty, and concern, but because we knew we were where God wanted us, we claimed the promise of Matthew 6:33. "But seek ye first the Kingdom of God and His righteousness, and all these things shall be added unto you." The Lord took over, and for the next four and a half years, we were never without what we needed.

God assured us of His involvement in our lives many times. One time my wife and I literally did not have any money to purchase groceries for the coming week. As we pondered the fact that we only had such things as salt and sugar, we sat together and prayed, not having any idea how God could resolve this. On the very day that we had used the last of the bread and peanut butter, we received a totally unexpected check in the amount we usually spent on groceries in a given week from a Sunday school class at my home church 1,000 miles away. This class never sent money before or after this, and it had been over a year since they had seen me.

God later led other churches to make unsolicited, budgeted financial commitments that helped us keep going when we had twins and then another child nineteen months later. My wife's boss randomly gave us $1,000 once, and another time he gave us several pieces of furniture that his brother had decided he no longer needed. Time and time again, we saw God provide for our needs through such generous acts of benevolence.

There were certainly times it was tempting to dwell on the fact that we did not have some things that other families had. It bothered me that we had to spend our savings and did not have any margin for emergencies. But then I would think about what the Lord was doing through our family and I had not only peace but a hilarious joy.

Experiences such as these are not exceptional among members of the body of Christ who have learned to completely trust the Lord with their finances. The happiness as a result of stewardship is open to every believer.

9

QUIET TIME

One trap that church members can fall into is the belief that the only time they need to spend on spiritual things is when they are at church. This is as absurd an idea as believing that the only time a child learns is when he is at school. Every teacher knows learning occurs both in the classroom and outside the walls of the school.

Even though a congregation may be blessed with an inspiring preacher and small group teachers, nothing can take the place of individual and personal Bible study and prayer. Members of the body of Christ who are truly happy consistently have a private, intimate relationship with the Lord that they foster through daily times of Bible study and prayer. Some make use of devotional guides, while others enjoy a personal study plan. Some set aside time in the morning, while others find it more productive to study in the evening. Whatever the hour and method, a personal time with God gives depth to a believer that cannot be obtained any other way.

Even with His busy ministry, Jesus Himself spent large amounts of time alone with God. His ministry began with a forty-day period of prayer and fasting alone. He often retreated from the crowds and sometimes even from His own disciples to have time alone with His Father, such as immediately following the feeding of the 5,000 when Jesus went to a mountain by Himself to pray (Matt. 14:23). At the end of His ministry, Jesus again found Himself alone, praying in the Garden of Gethsemane. If such times were important and necessary for Jesus, surely it is even more important and necessary that members of the body find regular times to build their relationship with God.

BIBLE STUDY

A strong, consistent time of studying Scripture can do wonders for any believer. Knowing what the Bible says about the issues one faces is a huge boost to a person's happiness level. Many people in our society have little more than popular opinion, feelings, advice of friends, and maybe the writings of secular gurus to guide them. Having the actual recordings of the mind of God is truly freeing in that these records are so dependable.

Being able to quote "My God shall supply all your need according to His riches in glory" (Phil. 4:19) has made a huge difference in my own life. As with most people, through the years, my own set of inadequacies and shortcomings surfaced along the way. For me, one of the biggest was extreme stage fright. For a person who felt called to the pastorate, this was a huge problem.

It all came to a head while I was preaching in front of five hundred people on a Wednesday evening at a large congregation in Louisiana. Ten minutes into the sermon, I literally passed out. The pastor did not know what else to do, so he gave the invitation—and three people came forward. (He later asked me if I could do it again and see if more would come!) This incident led to a time of doubt and questioning about my calling, as you might imagine. Here was a struggling ministerial student who could not get in front of a crowd to speak.

Help came from two big directions. One was a Christian counselor who led me to recondition myself by preaching sermons in front of a mirror, then to one person, then to a few people, etc. This was laborious, but it made a difference.

The second direction for help was Philippians 4:19. Over and over, I quoted this verse to myself. My need was unique and perhaps trivial to some but was overwhelming to me. As time went by, the security of knowing God could deliver me began to give me peace—in front of crowds and, as important, when I was alone. Over forty years later, I have preached approximately 6,000 times. In 2010 the Alabama Baptist Convention recognized me as Pastor of the Year. All of this was possible because of the power and peace of knowing the Word of God.

PRAYER

Members of the body of Christ, just like everyone else, have only so many waking hours in a day. We often find ourselves hurrying to get ready for work or school every morning. There is often just too much commotion to have a good prayer time before leaving. Once we arrive at work or school or wherever we spend our day, other matters demand our attention. One thing leads to another, and before we know it, the day is spent. Unless a believer is convinced that prayer is necessary for his personal growth, too many "important" things will crowd out any available time for him to spend with God.

Biographers record that Martin Luther, the German theologian, often rose at 4:00 a.m. so he would have adequate time to spend in prayer. When he was especially burdened with things to do and to address, he knew he needed to pray more, not less, and he did.

Acts 6 chronicles that a complaint emerged among the Hellenistic Christians who were part of the early church. Apparently, some thought the Gentiles were being overlooked in the daily distribution of food that the church prepared for the widows in the church.

Although they knew this complaint needed investigation, the apostles decided there were better uses of their time than overseeing this conflict resolution. They knew their main tasks of prayer and ministry would suffer if they spent too much time making sure the distribution was fair and equitable. So they set aside seven men to supervise the food allotments while they continued to pray and minister.

For any believer to be all God desires, he needs to do what these early leaders did and spend time in prayer. Prayer may easily be one of the most neglected areas in the lives of believers. Too often, prayer is seen as important but not vital. To be true to the examples in Scripture, a happy member of the body needs to spend an adequate amount of time alone in prayer with God.

One of the most trying times in my life was during my first pastorate. At the beginning of our second year at the church, my wife delivered premature twin girls. That summer, our church entered a building program, with much of the labor being volunteer. I was frequently finding myself bypassing a daily quiet time with God because I would get so busy trying to climb the mountain of issues that needed attention every day. When I did take time for prayer, it was often at 2:30 a.m. while half asleep and rocking a restless baby. "Surely God will understand" was my rationale. But I found that when I *did* take time for God, no matter what, that I had the most productive days.

At one point that year while I was still being taught this lesson, we had several volunteers scheduled to come from all over the state to help us frame up the church building. One week before they were to arrive, we still did not have the foundation poured because of difficulty getting our plumber to lay pipe, which had to be under the concrete. He was working hard on another job, and no matter how often I called, he just had not had time to come to our site. It began to look like we would have a bunch of volunteers sitting around for a week doing nothing. Thankfully, there were some members of our body who had sense enough to pray. That Wednesday night before the volunteers were supposed to arrive on Sunday, we prayed for the plumber for about an hour. God answered that prayer when on Thursday the plumber called us and said that though he could not come, he would send another fellow on the job Friday!

But this was not the end of the problem. When the other plumber finished his work that day, the inspector's air pressure gauge showed a leak. Such a leak could be almost impossible to find, especially not in the few minutes the inspector could wait. The plumber began to check the pipes, while a church member and I prayed. Miraculously, the plumber quickly found that a piece of tape used to plug a hole had come loose. The work passed inspection.

Now we had to find a way to get concrete poured on a Saturday. Again, it seemed an impossibility, but God was in control. On Sunday afternoon, we stood on green concrete as volunteers arrived. The Lord renewed His truth to me that I needed to take more time for conversation with Him, for there is so much He can do that I would never accomplish alone.

Still learning my lesson, within a few months, I was back to my old habits of sporadic time alone with God. I will never forget the evening when I walked in the door to find our baby girls in the living room, crying at the top of their lungs while trying to get out of their playpen that was keeping them captive. As they quieted, I heard a shrill cry from the basement. Rushing to the basement door, I opened it to find my wife, now quiet, climbing the stairs.

"I had had enough," she calmly said. "The girls have been fussing all night, and it was driving me insane! I went downstairs to let it out so I wouldn't scare the girls."

After getting the girls to sleep, my wife and I got together for something that we had not done nearly enough during the past year: prayer. This was not the most eloquent or most profound prayer either of us had ever prayed. To be honest, it was basically a prayer for relief! In many respects, this was a selfish prayer that night, but the girls slept all night for the first time in their nine months of existence. The next morning, not only was I deeply grateful for a full night's sleep, but I was also convicted about my need for a more consistent prayer life. I think the quiet night was my loving Lord reminding me how necessary it is to take quality time for Him.

QUIET TIME AND RELATIONSHIPS

Inevitably, something will happen to a member of a body of Christ that is not to his liking. A personality conflict may develop with another individual in the church, something may be said that is hurtful toward him or his family, his child may have trouble getting along with another child in the church, or the pastor may disappoint by falling into sin. The particulars will vary, but it is certain that anyone active in a body of Christ will face something that will disappoint or destroy his happiness within the body. If his happiness is based on circumstances or other's attitudes, then a member of the body is in for disappointments. On the other hand, if he has a strong, personal, daily relationship with the Lord, such instances, though trying, will not destroy his happiness.

One believer experienced one of her most difficult times while witnessing one evening. Upon returning after going out to share the gospel, believers had smiles on their faces and were excited about the opportunities they had to share about the Lord—everyone except one lady. When she was asked to share her experience with the group, this normally bubbly, happy lady almost broke into tears. She told how she and her partner stopped at one of their assigned houses and approached a man who was working outside. As they struck up a conversation with him, the man became harsh and vulgar and told them to leave.

The other folks who had been visiting tried to comfort this young lady who felt terrible as a result of her encounter. We prayed for her and for the man who had been so offensive. We also encouraged each other to pray for him in our private prayer times. As we left, I wondered what this would do to this lady's relationship to the church and to the Lord.

The following Sunday was a great time of worship. The young lady was there, trying to work through her disappointment and hurt from her visit that week. Imagine her surprise when the man who had been so rude was there as well. Seldom is prayer answered so visibly when our feelings are hurt, but God chose to bless this lady's obedience in the best way that Sunday morning. Many would have let their feelings get the best of them and avoid church altogether after such a perceived failure. But this lady's happiness grew because of her willingness to pray and persevere. Her joy was further increased within the month when the man accepted Christ and was baptized.

Of course, troubles and pressures that members of the body sometimes experience are not always so overt. Most issues are more subtle and thus harder to confront than was the case described above. Sometimes a member of the body has to cope with jealousies, gossip, half-truths, and deceit. These have been issues in churches since the beginning. In one of his letters to the Corinthian church, Paul wrote, "I fear lest when I come ... there be debates, envyings, wraths, strifes, backbitings, whisperings, swellings, tumults" (2 Cor. 12:20). James writes about quarrels and conflicts in the church. There are several passages that give ample evidence of rumors and backbiting between members of the body early on.

Scripture gives us directives on how the body of Christ is to handle situations like this. Titus 3:9–10 instructs believers to "avoid foolish questions ... and strivings about the Law; for they are unprofitable and vain. A man that is an heretic ... reject." Further guidelines are given in 2 Corinthians 13:1. "In the mouth of two or three witnesses shall every word be established." Other passages, such as Romans 16:17 and 1 Thessalonians 5:14, give even more direction.

But how does an individual member of the body respond to slander, gossip, or backbiting spoken against him? Attacks are often too subtle for there to be two or three witnesses. The truth is we know the answer. Jesus taught us to "love your enemies, do good to them which hate you, bless them that curse you, and pray for them which despitefully use you" (Luke 6:27–28). Who could be more of an enemy than one who spreads rumors, slanders, or reviles another?

Jesus also calls on a wronged member of His church to pray for the one doing the wrong. This does not mean that we should not confront the one doing wrong. In fact, Matthew 18:15–17 gives a strong precedent for going to one who has been hurtful. If a one-on-one meeting does not bring about change, then Scripture teaches that two or three others should be involved, and ultimately, the whole congregation should be brought in if necessary. But the attitude of the one who is wronged is key in the teachings of Jesus. In the rush to prove his innocence, the wronged person can forget to pray for his adversary. When this happens, the members of the body of Christ begin to look very much like those of the world.

Perhaps one of the most graphic instances in dealing with such things took place while I was still young in the ministry. After my wife gave birth to twins, one of the most surprising outcomes was a bit of notoriety in the small community. Instead of being "the pastor of Friendship Baptist Church," I became "the father of the twins who is pastor of Friendship Baptist Church."

During this time, I received a call from a man who had recently accepted the Lord and joined our church. He was concerned about his stepdaughter and her salvation. He asked that I come by and talk with her to see if I thought she understood what a commitment to the Lord would mean to her. I was there at the house, talking with the girl's stepfather when she arrived home after school. When she realized I had come to see her rather than her parents, she became obviously nervous and was finding it hard to open up enough to ask questions. I suggested to her parents that I could take her out for an ice cream cone and maybe that would help her be comfortable enough to be honest with me.

That early spring day was one that only those who have been cooped up for six months of a cold, snowy winter can appreciate. Close to the ice cream stand was a park where we went to take in this wonderful day and talk about the Lord and His salvation plan.

Right there among the glory of that beautiful day, this young girl accepted the Lord as her Savior. I took her back to her apartment, where she shared the good news with her parents. They were beyond happy. How could any problem possibly come out of this?

A few weeks later while visiting in the home of some prospects, I brought up the subject of their church membership. They had lived in our city for years but had never attended any church regularly. For a few months, they had occasionally visited our church and seemed to enjoy the fellowship, although they had not been there for a few weeks.

Their response was anything but expected. The wife hesitated, looked me over carefully, and then proceeded to tell me what she had heard. According to the grapevine, I had not only *one* set of twins but a second set of elementary-age illegitimate twins. She said I had been seen with them eating ice cream in the park recently. To say the least, no witnessing training had ever prepared me for that response.

Although there was not a shred of truth to this rumor, I could not convince this woman, and we never saw them in our church again. As I drove home, I tried to put together how this rumor could have started and realized someone must have seen me with the little girl I had taken to the park to talk about the Lord. By the time the story traveled through the rumor mill, the one girl had turned into twins, probably because of the recent birth of our daughters. What was so frustrating was that there was little way to fight such a rumor and no one to confront since I had no idea who had started it.

The best way to fight the frustration in such a situation was prayer. While it is not easy to pray for an unknown person who has hurt your reputation, prayer will make a big difference in being able to carry on. This kept an admittedly difficult situation from turning into an unbearable one.

In James 5:16 is a strong assertion about the power of prayer. "The effectual fervent prayer of a righteous man availeth much." Very often we see those accomplishments in terms of what happens in the world around us. That verse can also be taken to be speaking about what happens to a member of the body of Christ on the inside. A good prayer life is essential for happiness.

I am reminded of the time when a lady in our church approached me and wanted to pray for her relationship with one of her grown daughters, whom she had not heard from for a year. A week later when I saw her, she was ecstatic. Her daughter had called her "out of the blue." They talked for a significant amount of time, which is a huge step in restoring any relationship. It not only helped this lady to hear from her daughter, but her answered prayer helped to strengthen her faith as well. I was reminded that a fully happy believer needs to be consistently relying on a strong prayer life.

10

MUSIC

Music during worship is essential in the life of the body for the individual member to attain her happiness potential, regardless of her musical ability. Music helps to loosen inhibitions during worship, which leads to a closer relationship with God and thus increases the joy and happiness of the member who is participating. Music often provides a more conducive atmosphere for people to respond openly, whether that music is congregational singing or music being carried out by vocalists or instrumentalists with the congregation listening. The openness of spirit that is generated by worship music can have a tremendous effect on how open individual members of the body are to receiving and responding to the message and God's call on their lives.

Music comprised a critical element in the lives of several biblical characters. Paul wrote the Colossian Christians, telling them to teach and admonish each other with "psalms and hymns and spiritual songs" (Col. 3:16). Both Mary and Elizabeth have songs documented in the first chapter of Luke. Similarly, in the Old Testament, singing was a vital part of worship and celebration.

Moses celebrated the deliverance of the Hebrews at the Red Sea (Ex. 15:1–19) and extolled the providence of God (Deut. 32:1–43) with song. The prophetess Deborah in Judges 5 sang to celebrate the victory over Sisera. Hannah's song in 1 Samuel 2:1–10 is one of thankfulness for her son Samuel. Both the prophet Isaiah and King Hezekiah have songs recorded in the book of Isaiah. Of course, David and others have multiple songs that comprise the book of Psalms, including the songs used in the worship services of the ancient temple in Jerusalem.

MUSIC IN WORSHIP

Worship music has many elements, from solo performances to small group pieces all the way to entire congregations participating. Music that requires everyone's participation can often have the greatest impact on worshipers. Although the actual quality of music in congregational singing is not usually as great as when a trained musician performs, the participation element is a big key. The criteria for participation in congregational singing is never about ability; it is about the condition of the worshiper's heart. Faith, hope, and joy can be expressed and engendered as the body of Christ worships together in music. Someone fortunate enough to be a member of a body of Christ where the songs of the faith are joyfully sung by the congregation with willing and faithful hearts knows what a difference it makes to be a part of such a worship experience.

This principle was made clear to me, strangely enough, not in a church but while attending seminary. As I look back on those days, our chapel services are among the most unforgettable and heartwarming memories. Although we heard great preaching time after time, what I really remember from those services were the hymns we sang before preaching. The congregation was mainly comprised of men, and most did not have trained voices; but when those hymns were sung, it sounded like the roof had lifted and the angels were singing too. We sang without inhibition, without fear about being heard and ridiculed for lack of ability. Many times, I went to a chapel service while feeling overwhelmed by the pressures of so much to do and so little time in which to do it. Certainly, some sermons inspired me more than others, but it was the congregational singing that was a consistent source of encouragement. Being able to participate without inhibition brought me as close to the Lord as few other things could during those years.

Since that time, it has become apparent that how people respond after a church service is affected to a large degree by how much they feel a part of that service. Congregational singing is one of the few times that everyone can participate actively during worship. A well-chosen song can serve as a vehicle for the congregation to energetically praise the Lord from their hearts.

Years ago, the worship services at the church I pastored were just lacking something. No matter how hard I preached or how well the choir or soloists sang, the worship services seemed flat. The answer to the problem came from two very different sources: the Bible and a church softball team! The Bible is very plain that worship should involve all people from the congregation. There were not just two or three men doing all the talking, sharing, and singing in the New Testament church. Everyone had opportunity to be involved. That was where I had expected to find the answer, and this was certainly a major part of what needed to change.

A church softball team that was unfortunate enough to have me as a player helped me come to the same conclusion. We were definitely not the best team in our league, but we had loyal members who consistently showed up even if it was to get clobbered. Why did everyone keep showing up even though they knew there was a good chance we would lose? We all got to participate! Everyone who came got a chance to play. Because we had opportunity to take part, everyone was much more likely to be involved, supportive, and happy.

Carrying this concept into our worship services, we began

having people of all ages participate, especially during the singing, and new life was infused into our worship. Everyone who sang was by no means professional, but the general air of openness and spontaneity brought through the participation of so many in worship was a breath of fresh air.

MUSIC AND CRISES

Another aspect in which music can help a member of the body is when she is facing a crisis. How well an individual handles a calamity will affect her happiness level for months and sometimes years afterward. One of the elements faced in a tragedy is being able to express grief appropriately. Sorrow can be shown in many ways such as crying, talking, and even laughing on occasions. Those who bottle up their emotions at times of crisis are generally in store for more unhappiness, tension, and grief in the weeks and months ahead. Music has the ability to touch our emotions and allow them to be released, making it a very important tool in helping a member of the body of Christ vent the tensions, fears, and anxieties that accompany crisis situations.

Many times, in the pain of despair, a member of the body will recall the words of a hymn, a worship song, or a chorus more readily than even a verse of scripture. Whether it is because of the melodies associated with songs or some other reason, music can have a universal calming effect. Scripture mentions this phenomenon when Saul asks David to play the harp to quiet Saul's soul.

After a death, a funeral can be both traumatic and comforting to the families involved. Some funerals are more effective than others in not only helping those who attend to express their feelings but also in preparing them for new stages in life. Part of the difference is determined by what is said and how, but people express their emotions most during the music.

Not everyone sees the importance of music during a funeral. As a seminary student, one requirement of a course was to participate in a funeral service. I found a pastor who was willing to let me have a part in a funeral and who carried me along as he visited the family. The pastor was caring and seemed genuinely concerned, but he had little patience when the family expressed their grief. He was not fond of emotional, tearjerker songs. He thought it was inappropriate for a believer to make a scene at such a time; he thought they should be concentrating on the fact that the loved one was with the Lord.

Everything that was said before, during, and after the funeral was biblical, true, and even encouraging. Still, when all was said and done, the family felt like something had been missed during the process. I realized it was that the family had needed music so they could have had that avenue to express their sorrow in an understanding atmosphere. This principle has been reinforced by many people who have asked for a special song to be sung at their funeral or that of a loved one; they rarely ask for a particular sermon to be preached. The song generally is one that has meant something to them in times of crisis or times of worship, and it often has emotional overtones that may even bring some to tears.

In spite of the fact that there is grief, songs can bring contentment, peace, and closing that will lead to happiness in the days to come. Music has an amazing ability to help in this area like nothing else.

MUSIC AND JOY

Music not only helps members of the body find peace; it also helps them express the joy they have in the Lord. A happy member of the body of Christ needs avenues to express her joy. Although not every part of the charismatic movement from years ago was totally healthy, the jubilant singing that was part of that movement engendered joy in the Lord. A believer needs the opportunity to express that joy without creating confusion or chaos. Music can do this.

In the name of being true to orthodox beliefs and practices, too many church services have developed a stiff, conventional music style. Exuberant worship needs exuberant music that has accurate and true lyrics that touch the heart and mind. Effectively done, the music during worship can lead a member of the body to feel the joy of being God's chosen as nothing else can.

If a body of Christ has exhilarating, joyful, scriptural music in worship, the individual members are blessed. Few things touch our emotions like a song. Little else helps us feel the compassion our Lord has for His sheep. There are times a four-minute song can help us see the wonder of God's grace as well as a thirty-minute sermon. It is not possible for every member of a congregation to speak, preach, or teach at the same time, but everyone can lift their voices in praise together. Music and prayer are the two times in a worship time that everyone is participating. Involvement in worship can help each member feel a oneness with the other members of the body as well as with the Lord. As one person once told me, "I feel like I know more about heaven after a great song than any other time."

11

ENCOURAGEMENT

We are instructed to not forsake "the assembling of ourselves together" (Heb. 10:25) so that we might encourage one another. There really is a dynamic that encourages us when we receive confirmation from other people. This is seen in so many areas of our lives. For example, we see what a difference home court advantage makes in sports. All the way from professional football to local high school basketball, having supportive fans in the stands can make a significant difference in a team's confidence and ultimately in the score.

All of us have difficult periods in life where circumstances change, sometimes in an instant. Having even one or two people in our life to encourage us and help us get a positive perspective when the future looks bleak can make all the difference in having a good outcome. What better place than among a body of believers should we be able to find someone who can point the way to biblical counsel that reminds us of the power and grace of God? Every member of the body of Christ should be able to attest to how someone provided a word of encouragement at just the right time to pull him through a hard situation.

PURPOSEFUL ENCOURAGEMENT

There are different ways members of the body of Christ are encouraged, such as through a sermon, music, or an inspiring Bible study. But there is no substitute for having people encouraging each another with purpose. No matter how long a person has been a Christian, there will always be a need for encouragement. In 1 Corinthians 16:18, Paul writes that some fellow believers had come to him with the mission to refresh him. Certainly, if Paul needed this encouragement to regain some of his happiness, we do as well. In fact, biblically, it is evident that new believers and mature Christians alike need that extra boost that encouragement brings.

In the Old Testament, we read about Joseph when he had risen to be second-in-command in Egypt. He had a tremendous turnaround in his life, going from being incarcerated in Pharaoh's prison one day to being in charge of vast amounts of the country's wealth the next. He literally had the power of life or death over his brothers when they showed up to buy grain from Egypt's reserves. Of course, these were the brothers who had sold him into slavery years earlier. Because of their actions, Joseph had endured the indignity of being a servant and even being cast into prison unjustly.

Many a man in his position would have had his brothers killed or at least imprisoned or sold as slaves after how they had treated him. What Joseph did is quite amazing. He not only forgave them but invited them to live in the land of Goshen so they could be near him (Gen. 45:10). At least part of the reason for this was the encouragement Joseph knew he would get from his father, Jacob. In fact, when Jacob finally was able to make it to Egypt, Joseph fell on his father's neck (Gen. 46:29). This display of emotion helped both father and son restore their long-lost relationship.

There are many instances of members of the body of Christ encouraging each other in the New Testament. One of the most unusual happened when the first recorded instance of one being killed for his faith took place. Interestingly enough, it was a deacon, Stephen, who was the first martyr and not one of the apostles, although many of them were martyred later. Stephen was brought before the Sanhedrin, the council of the Jewish leaders. False witnesses were summoned and brought erroneous accusations against him. This is the same group that recently had Jesus put to death, so Stephen was well aware that he probably would meet the same fate.

We all understand the angst that such situations cause when we are the objects of false words that erode our credibility. What we find happening, however, is not an angry, defensive outburst on Stephen's part. Instead, he defends himself without including one word of criticism toward his accusers until the very end. There he does point to the fact that they were responsible for the death of "the Just One" (Acts 7:52). At this time, members of the council were "cut to the heart, and they gnashed on Him with their teeth" (Acts 7:54). It would be safe to say that a good word of encouragement would go a long way to help Stephen when surrounded by scores of those planning to kill him.

What happens next is unique and unexpected in that the Lord does not send a human messenger to let Stephen know of God's support. Instead, Stephen is allowed to see "the glory of God, and Jesus standing on the right hand of God" (Acts 7:55). This first Christian martyr was allowed to see into heaven and get a glimpse of not only where he was headed but Who would be there. The encouragement from such a vision had to give him a great amount of reassurance; it also served to properly warn his accusers.

The importance of well-given and well-timed encouragement was illustrated to me decades ago on an occasion when it was obvious that support had not been given. I had recently graduated from college and was preparing to go to seminary, and I enrolled in a ten-week chaplaincy program at one of our state's mental institutions. The first week the new students went with the older students as they conducted group sessions for some of the patients. I will probably never forget the trepidation I felt upon learning the next week would be my turn to lead a group session of my own.

Walking into the room the next week, about ten people stared at me from a small, cigarette-stained table. They all seemed to be fidgeting with a matchbox or looking down at the floor as if it were in danger of moving. It was obvious the ice needed to be broken quickly, so we went around the room while saying our names. As we were going around, one man took his opportunity to say more. "My name is John Potter [not his real name], and I used to lead the singing in a church back home, Preacher. I used to be a good Christian for a long time. Now I don't know about all that stuff."

As John continued, it became clear that he had run into some serious marital problems, and it appeared that John had put the blame for these problems on everybody but himself. Such a line of defense is very common. The problem is that if the fault lies elsewhere, then there is nothing one can do to make things better. By taking at least partial responsibility, John could have helped the situation because then he would have something to work on.

But apparently, no one in John's life at the time gave him any encouragement to either work on his problems or to let him know he and his marriage were both salvageable. Over the years, John had gotten down on his luck but, more crucially, down on himself. He turned to alcohol, which helped him forget for a while, but intensified his problems with his family. Soon his marriage ended, which sent him further down the ladder. John drifted with little purpose and direction, eventually finding himself in the institution where we were that day. The one thing John had developed was an ability to manipulate people's sympathy to get what he felt he needed. By this time, it was difficult to get him to genuinely open up so he could be genuinely helped.

What would have happened if there had been some member of

the body of Christ who supported, helped, and encouraged John in the early days of his marriage problems? How would his life had been different if a fellow believer had given him some guidance or had lifted him up? Unfortunately, no one did, and John slipped out of church life and slid away from a close relationship with the Lord.

PERSONAL NEED FOR ENCOURAGEMENT

As a pastor, there were times I not only needed to give encouragement but needed to receive it as well. Perhaps the most demanding time was when my wife and I took care of my elderly father. My mother passed away in a car accident nineteen years before Dad ultimately left us. After her death, Dad moved to our town to have family near, and for a long time he was fairly self-sufficient. My wife did his laundry, I kept up his yardwork, we cleaned his house, and we tried to spend some time with him. But by and large, he could still drive and take care of himself.

However, over the years, he started showing signs of senility. His forgetfulness slowly but surely grew worse and worse. When he was in public, whether it was adrenaline or a greater focus, he often did fine. Yet when he was relaxed and comfortable around us, his mind showed signs of slipping. This meant we had to be more involved in his life to try to keep him as safe as possible.

Many folks did not understand the extra time and concern we were having to dedicate to him, but thankfully a few did. There was a couple who lived close to my dad's house who often asked him over to eat or just to visit. They saw what was happening in Dad's life, and they would encourage us often. This was enormous in its effect on my well-being. Here my brain was telling me that no matter what, Dad had to be seen after. But it was so uplifting to have someone simply share what my wife and I already knew: that Dad's dementia was further along than most could see and that we had to be more involved in his life.

God called us to another church over three hundred miles away. This decision was extra difficult because of its effect on Dad. For a while, he did well and even stayed in the old community. Ultimately, he again realized he needed family close, so he found an affordable house a few houses down from ours. His close proximity made it especially easy to keep an eye on him.

As the years passed, he began to fade even more, both physically and mentally. In this new church family, there were those who helped encourage us and who encouraged him. That made all the difference. It became his daily routine to drive the short distance to the church and hang around the office break room. The staff did an exceptional job incorporating him into the comradery that usually is found in office situations.

When two hurricanes in two years hit our community, there was a massive amount of cleanup that needed to be done, including at Dad's house and ours. After days of hauling limbs, raking leaves, and cleaning up debris, we had created a one-hundred-foot-long pile near the road at our house. To say we were tired would be an understatement, for my wife and I were also working hard at our day jobs. But we still had to tackle Dad's yard. As we began again at Dad's, a couple from the church drove up with smiles on their faces, ready to dive in and help us clean the results of ninety-mile-per-hour winds on about twelve trees. They had just finished cleaning up their own yard and were as tired as we were. Words cannot express the encouragement that they brought that day.

After about five years, Dad could no longer live alone and had to move into our house so we could better care for him. He had begun having strokes and could not keep his medicine straight. For those who have been caregivers, the wear and tear such an arrangement creates for everyone concerned is immense. There are frequent unexpected incidents that disrupt everyone's routine, like when I came home for lunch one day and was greeted at the door by a hot blast of air. Immediately, I checked the thermostat and found it was eighty-three degrees inside the house. When I asked Dad what happened, he merely said, "It was a little cool to me so I thought I would take care of it."

There was also the time that one of the staff at the church brought a dozen doughnuts and put them in the break room for everyone to enjoy. Dad showed up that day about 10:00 a.m. as usual. About 11:00, I stopped by the room to take a break. Seeing the doughnut box, I thought I might have one, but there were only two left. After checking with everyone on staff, we discovered Dad had eaten ten doughnuts. He could not remember eating more than two, but he had plowed through almost the whole box. (And he still ate a hearty lunch that day!)

Through all this, there were members of the body of Christ who would invite us out, Dad included. They knew exactly what they were getting when they did this. The encouragement this meant to all of us was huge. In fact, as a pastor who had over a thousand members to uplift and encourage, it was because these folks poured into my cup that it was possible for me to pour into others.

Eventually, when it became a twenty-four/seven task to care for him, we had to put Dad into an assisted living facility. Still there were members of our church who not only visited my dad but who also continued to pump up my wife and me. Even when Dad had to go to the hospital for the last time, there was one nurse in the church who sat with him so I could take care of some administrative tasks. She was there when it was near the end and was able to use her training to make him as comfortable as possible.

It was through seeing all those who sent encouragement my way, and the rejuvenation it engendered in me, that the words of Matthew 25:40 really took on meaning. "Inasmuch as ye have done it unto one of the least of these my brethren, ye have done it unto Me." Jesus obviously is pleased as we give encouragement to whoever may need it. In fact, He identifies with those, no matter how overlooked, who could use a timely boost.

Over the years of ministry, it became obvious that everyone in a given church needs encouragement. In my early days, it seemed that there were some who were on top of things and others who needed care as well as encouragement. Looking back, it is apparent that every member of every church needs encouragement. It is those who give it as well as those who receive it in the midst of this plethora of need who begin to experience a greater joy.

12

DISCIPLESHIP

One of the big emphases in church life over the past few decades has been discipleship. Many programs have been developed to make sure new converts are not left floundering but are instructed in how best to follow Jesus. These are wonderful and fine. But there needs to be another step for new believers to be properly instructed and even truly happy. No matter their age, new Christians generally need advice about specific problems they are having that might not be covered by a program's materials. They might not even be covered by years of Sunday school lessons and sermons or even a book specifically on Christian growth and instruction. There are times that new Christians with alcohol or drug problems need to be specifically taught about the biblical principles pertaining to these matters. Others, whose families may be going through a divorce or with a family member with emotional issues, need to know what the Bible says about family life. New believers need to learn about sacrificial giving, which is usually a new concept for people coming out of the world. There was one occasion when I was called on to resolve the eternal destiny of a family pet. This was not trivial to the owners, and I was not aware of any discipleship program that even mentioned this. Certainly, there is no way a prewritten discipleship program can have all the answers to all the problems a new member of the body might have.

What is needed is a group of available leaders in a church who have enough biblical knowledge to give personal answers to personal questions. If the average member does not gain access to having her legitimate questions answered, her chances of faltering and missing out on the joy she might otherwise know are much greater.

One pastor related the experience he had had with a family he went to see who had stopped attending church. At one time they had displayed much zeal in serving the Lord. As it turned out, the problem was not that the church building was too hot, the preaching too cold, or the members too aloof. The issue was that one of the family's boys was becoming a discipline problem. The mother decided she did not want her unruly child to upset anything at church.

The pastor was able to show how Satan will use any and every tactic to lessen one's commitment to Christ. He was also able to reassure the parents, joke with the kids, and see the family brought back to their prior level of participation and joy in the Lord. Without this one-on-one visit about a specific problem, this happy ending likely would not have occurred. Whether it is a pastor, a deacon, a Sunday school teacher, a small group leader, or anyone else in a church body, these visits are necessary to help a church see its members fulfilled and happy.

BIBLICAL PRECEDENT

We often forget that in the wilderness, the people depended on Moses to be a judge for all their squabbles. He quickly learned that he could not adequately deal with all the issues coming his way in a fair and equitable manner. Exodus 18 tells us how Moses was being overly burdened trying to fulfill this one task. So he appointed "able men" to judge the disputes of the people. This way, each person had individualized treatment about his individual problems. Neither Moses nor any of the people were happy or satisfied when Moses was trying to do it all. By allocating his responsibility to other capable men, all concerned were able to enjoy a higher degree of relief and comfort. The system God led Moses to devise illustrates how the Lord wants His people to be treated as valued individuals and that their happiness is important to Him.

Many of the prophets in the Old Testament had students who followed them and learned from their actions. The best example of this is the way Elisha followed Elijah until Elijah was literally taken to heaven. Elisha's learning process was not carried on through classroom academics but through observing and interacting with one of God's great men. This personal touch enabled Elisha to have any questions he may have had amply addressed.

The New Testament takes this principle even further. Jesus Himself used one-on-one teaching extensively. The obvious example was that during the three years of His ministry, Jesus had twelve disciples who followed, listened, and learned. Even though they heard the greatest sermons ever preached, the twelve disciples still needed the individual attention Jesus gave them to mold them into the followers He desired. They needed explanations about the meaning of parables; they needed confirmation about the fidelity Jesus said marriage should have; they needed disciplining when it came to "jockeying" for positions in the kingdom of God. All of this individualized attention could not be given in a sermon. People need that personal word that expressly fits their own situation and understanding. When they receive it, they are much more likely to know true peace and joy.

A newer member of our church came to me with a personal problem. Just a few months earlier, this young man had had a tremendous conversion experience. By his own admission, he had been into drugs and alcohol very heavily. Then one day when he was on a drug trip, he had a strong sense that Satan was going to get him. The whole thing was terrifying.

He went to his father-in-law, who was a bivocational minister, and told him what had happened. In the presence of his father-in-law, this young man turned his life over to Jesus. What a difference! He gave up his wild lifestyle, he began treating his wife with respect, and he gained a sense of hope for his future.

Yet soon the young man's job, which had been lucrative, disappeared because of a drop in demand. He found himself unemployed and had to move in with his father-in-law. His wife found a job at night, which meant he had to watch their baby eight hours a day, a task that did him good but was more stressful than work. His life was headed the wrong way on many fronts, it seemed to him.

It was at this time that this young man and his wife visited our church. Over the next few weeks, he and I were able to get to know each other better, and he related much of his past. During our time together, I began to share about having faith in the Lord. After a time, this man was offered a good job, he was able to get a nice place for his family to live, and he regained much of his confidence. Most of all, he learned that the Lord will indeed take care of His children.

When a new Christian encounters some big problem, often she wrestles with it alone, feeling there is no one in the body in whom she can confide. The result is that a new believer can be discouraged because she cannot find a satisfactory solution on her own. This can be avoided by making sure each new believer has a shepherd who is close enough to her so proper instruction can be given on a personal basis. This shepherd can be a teacher, choir member, janitor, or any mature believer, as long as the person is open and willing to spend time to disciple.

BIG LIFESTYLE CHANGES

Some problems need a different kind of discipleship within the body if true happiness and resolution are to be found. Those who come to know Christ who are from very tough backgrounds often have huge lifestyle problems through which members of the body of Christ can help guide them. People with addictions generally need a tremendous amount of help, often including going to a rehabilitation institution for months. This is a long-term commitment for it is not usually the first rehabilitation when victory is truly won over substance abuse; it often takes multiple attempts before there is recovery.

It is not just down-and-out bums who have alcohol and drug problems. People from all strata of society are vulnerable. What is common is that anyone in the chains of addiction needs some personal accountability to win the victory. Of course she needs the power of Jesus more than ever, but she also needs a person or two who will push her to not only stay clean but also help her to change her lifestyle to really follow Jesus. Then and only then are true happiness and joy available.

Decades ago, I was asked to preach a revival at a men's home for recovering alcoholics and drug addicts. This became one of the highlights of my ministry. The first day, I got there early and was able to mingle with some of the guys before the service started. True to form, there were guys who, from their looks, had known some extremely tough times. There were others whose appearances portrayed richer lifestyles. In fact, I recognized one because he had been a quite famous athlete in professional sports. His face had been seen on TV for years. Yet here he was, one of those seeking help. He said this place had opened a door for him to regain hope and happiness. The hope came only after he made some big lifestyle changes.

Others have lived promiscuous lives along the way before they came to know Christ. To truly be happy, they have to learn to live out the biblical commands to offer their bodies as living sacrifices to God. When their addiction becomes so overwhelming, there are places that offer help for those with this kind of addiction. The help they offer includes guidance in making major changes in their lifestyles. Only when they begin to make those changes can they also begin to find the happiness they seek.

WHEN THE HONEYMOON
WITH JESUS WEARS OFF

While on the subject of discipleship, it should be mentioned that when a person becomes a Christian as well as a church member, there is often a time of jubilation and excitement. Many people have an experience like the lame beggar who was healed outside the temple after Peter commanded him to walk in the name of Jesus. He soon could be seen walking around, shouting for joy, and sharing with everyone the news of the changes in his life. It is also taught in Scripture that a close encounter with God is often followed by a period of trials and temptations. It was after Jesus was baptized and the Holy Spirit descended on Him that He was led into the wilderness to be tempted by Satan. During these periods of temptation, new members of the body are highly susceptible to self-doubt, enticements, and peer pressure. The wholehearted support of brothers and sisters in Christ at this time is essential.

Specifically, most churches experience a high dropout rate in involvement among new members within the first year of membership. One of the primary reasons is that a new believer will at some point hit a wall of discouragement about something for which she does not have an answer. Having a built-in system to make sure she can get a personalized answer for a personalized problem is a big factor in her continuing her journey with Christ with joy.

We get excited about a new baby and tell everyone we meet as we grin from ear to ear, but then comes the day-in and day-out battle of taking care of that baby. One cold January evening, my wife let me know it was time to go to the hospital to have our first child. This was several weeks before her due date, and we had not even begun our prenatal classes. At the hospital, several times nurses asked her about the validity of her due date, for she was definitely in labor. From 10:00 that night and through the next day, she worked through contractions. Finally, midway through the afternoon, the doctor decided to operate to remove the baby. He quickly went about his job, and a few minutes later, the delivery room was full of the sounds of a newborn's cries. Then he suddenly said, "Here's the problem! There's another one!" My wife asked, "Another what?" A short time later, the cries of two babies were filling the delivery room. (This was before ultrasounds were common as a part of prenatal care.) As I recovered from almost passing out, I did not go to the corner to mope, hide in the closet, or take a nap. It was tell-somebody time! We had just doubled the size of our family in one swoop, and who would not be excited? There was much for which to be thankful and good reason to be ecstatic.

Yet a few weeks later, those two babies came home. All of you who are parents know the rest of the story. The excitement died down, the presents and visits tapered off, and the day-to-day routine of caring for two infants settled in around us. There were continuous sleepless nights and dirty diapers. A parent, though proud, still has to endure some unsettling and unpleasant times.

What helped us immensely during those hard times were the one-on-one instructions from health care givers, parents, and friends. As all new parents do, we had many questions and issues that were not covered in any of the books we were devouring in our quest to be good parents. Without the personal guidance of caring and informed people who stepped up to "disciple" us, this time in our lives would have been close to unbearable.

The same can be said about new members of the body who are exploring this new area of church life. Planned programs are good. Yet there still need to be avenues for answering individual issues and concerns. With loving discipleship, a new member of the body has the potential to know true happiness.

EPILOGUE

"Isn't it great being a member of this church? I wish I could have just gotten here sooner!" These words summed up the feelings of a bright, vivacious person. Such enthusiasm about one's church does not have to be unusual. In fact, in looking at the early church, this feeling was quite normal.

Following and internalizing the secrets in this book will allow all of us to know joy and happiness from our church life.

Printed in the United States
by Baker & Taylor Publisher Services